➢ DC–LD

[Diagnostic criteria for psychiatric disorders for use with adults with learning disabilities/mental retardation]

Royal College of Psychiatrists

Occasional Paper OP48

Gaskell
London

Gaskell is an imprint of the Royal College of Psychiatrists
17 Belgrave Square, London SW1X 8PG

British Library Cataloguing-in-Publication Data
A catalogue record for this book is available from
the British Library.
ISBN 1-901242-61-7

Distributed in North America
by American Psychiatric Press, Inc.

CONTENTS

Contents

Figures

PREFACE

The impetus for the development of DC–LD arose from a group of academic learning disability psychiatrists. We wanted to improve upon existing general population psychiatric diagnostic classificatory systems for use with adults with learning disabilities. Following debate within the Penrose Society (the UK learning disabilities research group for doctors), an initiative was established to collaborate with the Royal College of Psychiatrists to develop an improved classificatory system. This collaboration has produced DC–LD, which reflects a consensus of current practice and opinion among learning disabilities psychiatrists in the UK and Republic of Ireland. Production of DC–LD is not meant to be the final statement as to how psychiatric disorders and problem behaviours present in this population, but a starting point, to inform and facilitate clinical practice and research. Hence, DC–LD describes criteria that will hopefully evolve and be improved upon over time as our knowledge-base and experience expand.

Whereas DC–LD might be viewed as a 'stand-alone' classificatory system for use with adults with moderate to profound learning disabilities, its use should be seen as complementary to the ICD–10 manuals for people with mild learning disabilities. Hence, the DC–LD and ICD–10 manuals may be used side-by-side, depending upon the particular circumstances of the individual. The development of DC–LD has drawn extensively upon the ICD–10 manuals, and attempts have been made throughout DC–LD to cross-reference with the ICD–10 manuals, to enable a complement-ary approach to be taken, particularly with adults with mild learning disabilities. Throughout DC–LD, cross-reference is also made to the nearest equivalent DSM–IV codes.

DC–LD is not an interviewing instrument, nor does it attempt to explain the aetiology of psychiatric disorders or problem behaviours, which vary in individual cases. It is purely a classificatory system providing operationalised diagnostic criteria. As such, it will hopefully be of value in providing research diagnoses, where clarity and precision are required with regard to the exact disorder being studied (i.e. standardised diagnostic criteria), so that direct comparisons may be made between studies and between groups within studies. DC–LD may also be of value in enhancing clinical practice, as descriptive diagnosis is an important step prior to elucidating aetiology and then developing appropriate plans for treatments/interventions/supports.

In clinical practice, 'partial syndromes' sometimes present and clinical judgement in such circumstances is important. Clinicians must develop a diagnostic working hypothesis even when exact DC–LD criteria are not met, in order to offer constructive help to the individual and his or her family/carers. Sometimes these hypotheses evolve or change over time, as the nature of the person's needs becomes clearer. In these cases of partial syndromes, DC–LD should not be viewed as a hindrance to clinical practice. The term 'DC–LD depressive episode' implies that the exact criteria are met. However, if the person has, for example, only three instead of four of the relevant depressive symptoms, but his or her presentation is judged to more closely resemble this diagnostic group than others, it would be reasonable for a skilled clinician to assume 'possible/probable DC–LD depressive episode' as a working hypothesis. This would then inform treatment choices: subsequently, the diagnosis could be upheld or revised in the light of further information gained over time. Such decisions require clinical training, skill and experience.

The inclusion within DC–LD of the categories for personality disorders and problem behaviours (which are purely descriptive rather than implying any understanding of causation) might be viewed as controversial. These categories were included only after considerable debate, and following feedback from the piloting/consultation process. It is recognised that further work will be required to better understand the aetiologies of such presentations: inclusion within DC–LD might facilitate such work. The supplementary categories within DC–LD Level D: Problem behaviours are optional, for use by those clinicians who find them helpful.

Many individuals have contributed to the development of DC–LD, either through contributing to the existing literature on psychopathology and psychiatric disorders in adults with learning disabilities, or more specifically by contributing to the coordinated DC–LD piloting/consultation process as one of the field centres across England, Northern Ireland, the Republic of Ireland, Scotland and Wales. With the criteria now more widely available for clinical and research use, this work will hopefully be built upon in future years.

Sally-Ann Cooper, Chair of the DC–LD Development Working Group

CAUTIONARY NOTE

! These diagnostic criteria are intended to facilitate the diagnosis of psychiatric disorders occurring in adults with learning disabilities/mental retardation, to improve diagnostic agreement among clinicians, and to aid communication. It is hoped that they will facilitate clinical practice and research. The criteria are believed to represent a consensus of professional opinion in the UK and Republic of Ireland. DC–LD does not include all conditions for which people with learning disabilities/mental retardation may be treated. Research evidence concerning the classification and nosological status of many of the disorders included is at a very early stage, and it is expected that these criteria may need to be revised in the light of further research. The inclusion of a diagnostic category within the DC–LD classificatory system does not imply that the condition necessarily is a medical disease, impairment, disability or mental disorder. The criteria may not be relevant to legal issues, or decisions about matters such as responsibility for acts, capacity, competence, disability or fitness to stand trial in particular jurisdictions.

DC–LD DEVELOPMENT WORKING GROUP MEMBERS

Dr Nicola M. Bailey, Specialist Registrar in Learning Disabilities Psychiatry, Oxford Deanery Higher Training Scheme, Oxford

Dr David J. Clarke, Consultant Psychiatrist in Learning Disability, Lea Castle Centre, Kidderminster

Professor Sally-Ann Cooper, Chair of the DC–LD Development Working Group, Professor of Learning Disabilities and Honorary Consultant in Learning Disabilities Psychiatry, Department of Psychological Medicine, University of Glasgow

Dr Shaun Gravestock, Consultant Psychiatrist and Honorary Senior Lecturer in Mental Health of Learning Disabilities, Oxleas NHS Trust, London

Dr Anthony J. Holland, Lecturer and Honorary Consultant Psychiatrist, Department of Psychiatry, Developmental Psychiatry Section, University of Cambridge

Dr Helen Matthews, Consultant Psychiatrist, Pembrokeshire and Derwen NHS Trust, Carmarthen

Professor Gregory O'Brien, Professor of Developmental Psychiatry and Honorary Consultant Psychiatrist, University of Northumbria

Dr Neill Simpson, Consultant Psychiatrist, Borders Primary Care NHS Trust, Roxburghshire

DC–LD CONSULTATIVE GROUP MEMBERS

Dr Paul Addison, Consultant in Learning Disabilities Psychiatry, North West Anglia Health Care Trust, Norfolk

Dr Regi Alexander, Consultant Psychiatrist, Leicestershire and Rutland Health Care NHS Trust, Leicester

Dr Timothy Andrews, Consultant in Learning Disabilities Psychiatry, Oxford Learning Disability NHS Trust, Oxford

Dr Val Anness, Consultant Psychiatrist, Bro Morgannwg NHS Trust, Mid Glamorgan

Dr Jane Bernal, Consultant in Learning Disabilities Psychiatry, Joan Bicknell Centre, London

Dr Harm Boer, Consultant in Learning Disabilities Psychiatry, North Warwickshire NHS Trust, Birmingham

Dr Johnston Calvert, Chairman of the Irish Division of the Royal College of Psychiatrists, Dublin

Dr Geraldine Cassidy, Consultant in Learning Disabilities Psychiatry, North Warwickshire NHS Trust, Birmingham

Dr Richard Collacott, Consultant Psychiatrist, Western Isles Hospital, Stornoway

Dr Leila Cooke, Consultant Psychiatrist, Bath and West Community NHS Trust, Bristol

Dr Sherva Cooray, Consultant Psychiatrist/Honorary Senior Lecturer, Parkside Health, Kingsbury, and Imperial College, University of London

Dr Ken Courtenay, Specialist Registrar in Learning Disabilities Psychiatry, Department of Psychiatry of Disability, St George's Hospital Medical School, University of London

Dr Marietta Cunningham, Specialist Registrar in Psychiatry, North and West Belfast Health and Social Services Trust, Antrim

DR SHOUMI DEB, Senior Lecturer and Honorary Consultant Psychiatrist, Department of Psychiatry, University of Wales

DR FIONA FARQUHAR, Senior House Officer, Ely Hospital, Cardiff

DR DLER FARRAJ, Consultant Psychiatrist, North Birmingham NHS Trust, Birmingham

DR BRIAN FITZGERALD, Consultant Psychiatrist, Enfield Community Care NHS Trust, Enfield

DR ANGELA HASSIOTIS, Senior Lecturer and Honorary Consultant Psychiatrist, Department of Psychiatry, University College London Medical School, University of London

DR FABIAN HAUT, Specialist Registrar in Psychiatry, Tayside Primary Care NHS Trust, Dundee

DR JOHN HILLERY, Consultant Psychiatrist, Stewart's Hospital, Dublin

DR SUSAN JOHNSTON, Senior Lecturer/Consultant Psychiatrist, School of Health and Related Research, Section of Forensic Psychiatry, University of Sheffield

DR TERRY JONES, Consultant Psychiatrist, Pembrokeshire and Derwen NHS Trust, Pembrokeshire.

DR JAS LIDHER, Specialist Registrar in Learning Disabilities Psychiatry, North Warwickshire NHS Trust, Birmingham

DR JANET MACPHERSON, Consultant Psychiatrist, North and West Belfast Health and Social Services Trust, Antrim

DR CAROLINE MARRIOTT, Consultant Psychiatrist, North and West Belfast Health and Social Services Trust, Antrim

DR DOROTHY MARSDEN, Specialist Registrar in Learning Disabilities Psychiatry, Learning Disabilities Service, Middlesborough

DR JANE MCCARTHY, Consultant Psychiatrist/Senior Lecturer, Department of Psychiatry, Newcastle University

DR KELLEY MCCARTNEY, Specialist Registrar in Psychiatry, North and West Belfast Health and Social Services Trust, Antrim

DR JUSTINE MCCULLOCH, Senior House Officer, Tayside Primary Care NHS Trust, Dundee

Dr Robin McGilp, Consultant Psychiatrist, Greater Glasgow Primary Care NHS Trust, Glasgow

Dr Maria McGinnity, Consultant Psychiatrist, North and West Belfast Health and Social Services Trust, Antrim

Dr Craig Melville, Specialist Registrar in Psychiatry, West of Scotland Higher Training Scheme, Glasgow

Dr Parva Nayer, Consultant Psychiatrist – Learning Difficulties, City and Hackney Community Services NHS Trust, London

Dr Kerry Ng, Staff Grade Psychiatrist, North and West Belfast Health and Social Services Trust, Antrim

Dr Verinder Prasher, Consultant and Senior Clinical Lecturer – Neurodevelopmental Psychiatry, Northern Birmingham Community NHS Trust, Birmingham

Dr Adrienne Regan, Consultant in Learning Disabilities Psychiatry, Harrow Learning Disabilities Team, Stanmore

Dr Lisa Rippon, Specialist Registrar in Psychiatry of Learning Disabilities, Prudhoe Hospital, Northumberland

Dr Ashok Roy, Consultant in Learning Disabilities Psychiatry, North Warwickshire NHS Trust, Birmingham

Dr Manga Sabaratnam, Consultant in Learning Disabilities Psychiatry, Hounslow and Spelthorne Community and Mental Health NHS Trust, London

Dr Marian Seager, Specialist Registrar in Learning Disabilities Psychiatry, Northgate Hospital, Northumberland

Dr Oliver Shanks, Consultant Psychiatrist, North and West Belfast Health and Social Services Trust, Antrim

Dr William Thompson, Consultant in Learning Disabilities Psychiatry, Pembrokeshire and Derwen NHS Trust, Carmarthen

Dr Vicky Turk, Consultant Clinical Psychologist and Lead Clinician, Oxleas NHS Trust, London.

Dr Joseph Vella, Specialist Registrar in Learning Disabilities Psychiatry, North Warwickshire NHS Trust, Birmingham

INTRODUCTION

The relationship of DC–LD to ICD–10 and DSM–IV

Diagnostic Criteria for Psychiatric Disorders for Use with Adults with Learning Disabilities/Mental Retardation (DC–LD) is a new classificatory system that has been developed in recognition of the limitations of the ICD–10 manuals (*ICD–10 Classification of Mental and Behavioural Disorders – Clinical Description and Diagnostic Guidelines* (ICD–10–CDDG; World Health Organization (WHO), 1992), *ICD–10 Classification of Mental and Behavioural Disorders – Diagnostic Criteria for Research* (ICD–10–DCR; WHO, 1993), and *ICD–10 Guide for Mental Retardation* (ICD–10–MR; WHO, 1996)) and the *Diagnostic and Statistical Manual of Mental Disorders, Fourth Edition* (DSM–IV; American Psychiatric Association, 1994). These limitations relate to certain psychiatric disorders that present differently in adults with learning disabilities, compared with adults of average ability. DC–LD should be viewed as complementary to the ICD–10 manuals, with the two sets of criteria employed alongside each other. When appropriate, ICD–10 criteria should be employed. This may be the case for some (but not all) adults with mild learning disabilities. Where DC–LD criteria appear more appropriate for the individual in question, they should be employed. This is likely to be the case for adults with moderate to profound learning disabilities. DC–LD does not describe the full range of psychiatric disorders; it addresses disorders more commonly found in this special population where existing ICD–10 criteria are inadequate. For example, problem behaviours and attention-deficit hyperactivity disorder of adults (ADHD) are described, whereas psychiatric disorders associated with the use of alcohol and drugs are not. The DC–LD framework makes reference to these latter disorders, but indicates that ICD–10 criteria should be used. The diagnostic criteria developed in this document are for use with adults with learning disabilities; they are not appropriate for use with children. It is recommended that DC–LD is adopted routinely in clinical and particularly research use.

The structure of DC–LD reflects the fact that its prime focus is to describe diagnostic criteria for psychiatric disorders (those disorders included on 'Axis III – Associated Psychiatric Disorders' in ICD–10–MR). However, listing Axes I ('Severity of Learning Disabilities') and II ('Causes of Learning Disabilities') within the document is essential, as such knowledge influences diagnosis in some cases. Examples include diagnosis of ADHD (see page 70–71) and the diagnosis of symptoms of abnormal eating in a person with Prader-Willi syndrome (see page 12). DC–LD also includes three appendices for users' convenience. The three appendices are:

- A new section detailing brief descriptions of learning disabilities syndromes and behavioural phenotypes.

- An outline of disorders included in ICD–10 Chapters other than V (similar but more extensive than those listed as 'Axis IIB: Other Associated Medical Conditions' in ICD–10–MR, annexed as 'Other Conditions From ICD–10 Often Associated with Mental and Behavioural Disturbance' in ICD–10–CDDG, but not included in ICD–10–DCR).

- An outline of ICD–10 Chapter XXI: Factors Influencing Health Status and Contact with Health Services (similar to that listed as 'Axis V: Associated Abnormal Psychosocial Situations' in ICD–10–MR, annexed as 'Other Conditions From ICD–10 Often Associated with Mental and Behavioural Disturbance' in ICD–10–CDDG, but not included in ICD–10–DCR).

These three sections are appendixed rather than forming part of the main body of DC–LD, in recognition of the prime focus of DC–LD in delineating operationalised diagnostic criteria for psychiatric disorders. Figures 1–3 demonstrate how the structure of DC–LD relates to that of the ICD–10 manuals and DSM–IV, and how the ICD–10–MR relates to DC–LD, ICD–10–CDDG and to DSM–IV .

The process of development of DC–LD

DC–LD has been developed by a network of learning disabilities psychiatrists working in the UK and Republic of Ireland. It describes consensus diagnostic criteria for psychiatric disorders as they present in adults with learning disabilities. It has not been developed for use with children. It is intended for use by practising psychiatrists and other health professionals who have been trained in clinical diagnosis, and can be used alongside the ICD–10 manuals. DC–LD was developed on behalf of the Penrose Society and the Faculty for the Psychiatry of Learning Disability of the Royal College of Psychiatrists. A working group was established, with a further consultative group contributing to the development process, in order to refine the criteria through a piloting procedure. The members of the two groups are widespread and currently practising in England, Northern Ireland, the Republic of Ireland, Scotland and Wales. The working group additionally consulted the published literature on psychiatric diagnostic criteria and relevant issues in adults with learning disabilities, to review existing international opinion and evidence, in order to inform the process of developing criteria. The work drew heavily upon existing diagnostic criteria for use with the general population published as the ICD–10 manuals. However, the criteria derived essentially reflect current practice within the UK and Republic of Ireland.

All of the new operationalised criteria presented in Axis III have been piloted via the field centres across the UK and Republic of Ireland, with the exception of dementia in Huntington's disease, acute stress reaction and anankastic personality disorder. Piloting of clinical presentation was undertaken with individuals in receipt of learning disabilities psychiatric care and across the full range of severity of learning disabilities. The following number of individuals met DC–LD criteria in the specified categories: pervasive developmental disorders – 74; dementias – 15; delirium – 4; non-affective psychotic disorders – 71; affective disorders – 101; neurotic and stress-related disorders – 52; eating disorders – 14; hyperkinetic disorders – 9; personality disorders – 39; and specific subtypes of problem behaviours (not including the supplementary categories for problem behaviours) – 319. Other ICD–10 disorders were present in 11 cases. The piloting/consultation process provided a consensus view of good face validity for the DC–LD criteria against clinical diagnosis.

CODING AND RECORDING

DC–LD codes are provided for each disorder/behaviour. These have been developed as a 'shorthand' that may be of use, for example, in computerised databases. DC–LD also cites the relevant F codes from the three ICD–10 manuals in the introductory section to each group of psychiatric disorders, and in its contents listings. Similarly, it provides the nearest equivalent DSM–IV code. Following the name of each DC–LD category, ICD–10 codes are listed in brackets, followed by DSM–IV codes in separate brackets. The cited ICD–10 and DSM–IV codes relate to those disorders that are most closely equivalent to the disorders described in DC–LD. This is in order to facilitate cross-referencing between the five documents. For some DC–LD disorders/behaviours, there are no equivalent ICD–10 and /or DSM–IV disorders, and so no equivalent ICD–10 and/or DSM–IV code can be given. Within DC–LD Axes I ('Severity of learning disabilities'), II ('Causes of learning disabilities') and III Level A ('Developmental disorders'), all but one of the disorders listed are exact ICD–10 disorders (i.e. DC–LD has not modified the ICD–10 diagnostic criteria). Consequently, in these three sections the codes are exact, rather than being close equivalents.

The type of information recorded in any summary statement of a person's health will depend upon the aims of the research/clinical service, and personal choice. DC–LD describes diagnostic criteria for psychiatric disorders only, as physical disorders are already well delineated. In some cases, a summary statement will need to include information on the person's physical disorders/disabilities in addition to his or her psychiatric disorders. For this reason, a list of codes from ICD–10 chapters other than V is included in Appendix 2.

Appendix 3 provides a list of factors influencing health status and contact with health services, taken from ICD–10 Chapter XXI. This information is included for those who find it helpful. It is important to be aware that ICD–10 states that codes from this chapter should not be used for international comparison. The areas covered in this appendix/chapter do *not* provide a comprehensive listing of all aetiological factors for psychiatric disorders. Researchers/clinicians may find other frameworks more helpful, such as considering factors under the four broad headings of:

1   Biological/physical factors
2   Psychological factors
3   Social factors
4   Factors related to developmental level.

An alternative model is to consider aetiology of psychiatric disorders under the headings of:

1   Predisposing factors
2   Precipitating factors
3   Maintaining factors.

It can also be useful to consider these two aetiological frameworks together in matrix form, whereby biological, psychological, social and developmental factors are all considered under each of the three headings of predisposing, precipitating and maintaining factors. Most textbooks of psychiatry discuss these issues in more detail, and should be referred to for further information. Appendix 3/ICD–10 Chapter XXI does not allow for this level of detail, comp-rehensiveness or flexibility. This limitation is acknowledged and appropriate caution is required (as listing codes from Appendix 3/Chapter XXI that do not fully account for the recognised aetiology will provide some information about the person, but may present a biased view of aetiology and hence of the person's health needs).

Which summary information is documented is at the discretion of the individual researcher/clinician, and will depend upon the purpose of the work. Figure 4 shows a format taken from clinical practice, but other researchers/ clinicians will need to adopt their own format to meet the aims of their service/work.

DIAGNOSIS OF PSYCHIATRIC DISORDERS IN ADULTS WITH LEARNING DISABILITIES

Accurate psychiatric diagnosis is an essential step in the management of an individual's mental health needs. It guides the clinician as to which treatments/interventions/supports are likely to be appropriate for that adult, and confers some information about likely prognosis. It is a 'shorthand' description of an adult's presentation and needs. Accurate diagnosis is also important in psychiatric research, which is needed to expand the evidence-base and to develop the most effective treatment plans.

The stages of psychiatric diagnosis

The psychiatric assessment involves three stages. This is equally true for diagnosis among adults with learning disabilities as it is for other adults.

1 Collect all the relevant psychopathology. This involves listening to the adult with learning disabilities and to his or her carers/relatives as they describe the symptoms and needs of the person. Following this, specific questions must be asked about the full range of psychopathology that may present in psychiatric disorders, in order to determine which symptoms and traits are, and which are not, present. It is always important to take a clinical history from an informant (i.e. a carer or relative) as well as from the adult with learning disabilities.

2 Clusters/patterns of psychopathology tend to occur together in diagnostic groups. The psychopathology is classified into these diagnostic groups using the diagnostic criteria. This is the descriptive diagnosis.

3 The aetiology of the descriptive diagnosis is determined through a combination of clinical history-taking, mental state examination, physical examination and special investigations. Aetiology of psychiatric disorders is usually

described under the sub-headings 'physical', 'psychological', 'social' and 'developmental'. Sometimes, the additional framework of 'predisposing', 'precipitating', and 'maintaining' aetiological factors is employed.

> *This document focuses on Stage 2 of this process: diagnostic criteria*

Additional considerations regarding psychiatric diagnosis in adults with learning disabilities that have led to the development of DC–LD

When conducting psychiatric assessments with adults with learning disabilities, special considerations in addition to those required when assessing someone of average ability are needed. This is the case at both Stages 1 and 2 of the stages of psychiatric diagnosis listed above.

At Stage 1 of the assessment, special care has to be taken in eliciting the psychopathology. This is because some adults have limited communication skills, and may have difficulty explaining their symptoms. They may also have difficulty understanding questions. Questions must be asked in simple language, using short sentences, appropriate to the adult's developmental level. The assessor must be aware of the possibility of the adult being suggestible and giving compliant answers, for example, the person answering 'yes', or repeating the last word or phrase when given a choice of alternatives. Questions and answers need to be repeated and checked out. As far as possible, the adult should be allowed to give an account in his or her own words, with the use of 'open' and non-leading prompts, prior to clarification and more direct questioning. Even the most able adult with learning disabilities is likely to have difficulty with some parts of the assessment process, such as remembering and describing the sequence of events and timescales. For this reason, it is always important to additionally complete an assessment with a carer/relative, preferably with a person who knows the adult with learning disabilities well, and who has known them for the longest period of time (e.g. a parent). Sometimes it is necessary to collate assessment details from several informants.

There may be limitations in taking a history from an informant. Sometimes, background information is not available, for example, if the adult has lost contact with or is bereaved of his or her parents and has moved to a new home in another part of the country. In order to demonstrate change in an adult's psychopathology (i.e. to distinguish psychiatric symptoms from longstanding traits), information regarding his or her premorbid state is essential, but not always available. Additionally, informants do not always have detailed information about the adult's current presentation – this depends upon many factors, such as how observant and experienced the carers are, how much individual time they spend with the adult with learning disabilities, and how well information is shared between different carers. Occasionally, an informant may bring his or her own personal bias into descriptions.

Having collected the psychopathology as described in Stage 1 above, Stage 2 of the diagnostic process is to classify it using diagnostic criteria. However, standard diagnostic criteria developed for use with the general population, for example the DSM–IV and the ICD–10 manuals, are not appropriate for use with adults with learning disabilities with regard to some disorders. This is particularly so for those with moderate to profound learning disabilities. The three main limitations of these diagnostic systems are:

1   Adults with learning disabilities do not experience the same range of psychopathology within disorders as people of average ability experiencing the same disorder (i.e. clinical presentation of psychiatric disorders differs in those with more severe learning disabilities). Examples of such a difference include onset of/increase in aggression or other problem behaviours. This is a common symptom of psychiatric illness in adults with learning disabilities, but not among adults of average ability.

2   General population psychiatric diagnostic criteria are weighted towards verbal items (rather than easily observable items) and intellectually complex concepts, which require a certain developmental level to have been attained (e.g. death, guilt, body image). Some general population criteria include changes in social functioning that are also difficult to apply in their existing format, given the differing baseline functioning of adults with learning disabilities.

3   DSM–IV and the ICD–10 manuals provide detailed sub-categories and related categories within diagnostic groups. Given the limitations in eliciting psychopathology described above (both with regard to the communication skills of the adult with learning disabilities, and difficulties with informant histories), it seems inappropriate to subdivide diagnostic categories to the same extent as for the general population. Greater subdivision is likely to introduce inaccuracy and lessen validity, for example, with regard to types of dementia or non-affective psychotic disorders.

In view of these limitations at Stage 2 of the diagnostic process, work was undertaken to develop diagnostic criteria for psychiatric disorders as they present in adults with learning disabilities: DC–LD. It describes consensus diagnostic criteria; a consensus of the current diagnostic practice of learning disabilities psychiatrists in the UK and Republic of Ireland. Such psychiatrists have undertaken specialist general psychiatric training, and higher training in learning disabilities psychiatry, and have been deemed to have attained an appropriate standard, through examination, by the Royal College of Psychiatrists. Learning disabilities psychiatrists in the UK and Republic of Ireland carry individual case-loads as well as supervising/advising psychiatrists in training, other health professionals, and psychiatrists working in other psychiatric specialities. As such, there is a considerable body of clinical experience held within the group. Hence, this addresses the need for face validity of any diagnostic criteria that are developed. Validity is the key issue at Stage 2 of the diagnostic process, which is the stage addressed by DC–LD. In contrast, reliability is key at Stage 1 of the diagnostic process (i.e. the reliability of elicitation of each individual item of psychopathology that is measured): this is dependent upon the training and skill of the assessor, and may be aided by the use of semi-structured psychiatric rating scales (to reduce the likelihood of particular items being omitted from the assessment). Consequently, DC–LD is only recommended for use by practising psychiatrists and health professionals who have been trained in clinical diagnosis, as it assumes an appropriate level of reliability at Stage 1.

SPECIAL ISSUES IN DEVELOPING DC–LD

ICD–10 'organic' disorders

The ICD–10 manuals classify some disorders on the basis of presumed aetiology, in categories F06 and F07 (described as 'Other mental disorders due to brain damage and dysfunction and to physical disease', and 'Personality and behavioural disorders due to brain disease, damage and dysfunction'). However, these categories should not be used purely because the person has learning disabilities, or an identified learning disabilities syndrome, or epilepsy. Such an assumption regarding aetiology should not be made because, for example:

1   Some psychiatric disorders currently not listed as such may have an organic aetiology, for example, schizophrenia may be a neurodevelopmental disorder. This is an issue for diagnostic criteria use with the general population, but is particularly so for adults with learning disabilities. Schizophrenic/delusional episode appears to occur at three times the general population rate in adults with learning disabilities. Presumably this (at least in part) relates to organic factors, for example, genetic abnormalities and brain damage. However, the DC–LD working group elected to use the term schizophrenic/delusional episode in preference to organic hallucinosis, etc.

2   When psychiatric disorders are of organic aetiology, other aetiological factors (psychological, social, developmental and physical factors other than the identified organic aetiology) may still be important in predisposing, precipitating or maintaining the clinical presentation. For example, an adult with a mood disorder associated with head injury is still vulnerable to the effects of a superimposed urine infection, significant life events, and whether his or her background during the developmental phase was disadvantaged or not. In view of this, the DC–LD working group considered it inappropriate to diagnose purely on the basis of the person having

learning disabilities, that is, just *one* of the relevant aetiological factors. Hence, the ICD–10 organic disorders categories F06 and F07 should not be used purely because the adult has learning disabilities (or an identified learning disabilities syndrome or epilepsy). Instead, the appropriate DC–LD Axis III category should be used.

The organic classificatory criteria may be appropriately used where there is an *additional* clear organic aetiology identified, for example urinary tract infection and thyroid dysfunction. In such cases, the organic factor should be temporally related to the onset of psychopathology, and the psychopathology should resolve with treatment of the organic pathology.

Behavioural phenotypes

Classification of psychiatric disorders on the basis of presumed aetiology is furthered flawed when considering adults with learning disabilities, in view of the concept of behavioural phenotypes.

There is increasing recognition of the behavioural phenotypes of some causes of learning disabilities: for example, Down's syndrome is associated with dementia, and Prader-Willi syndrome may be associated with psychosis. Does this mean that if an adult with Down's syndrome develops dementia it would be assumed aetiologically to be dementia of Down's syndrome? Clearly not, as it would be important to investigate and exclude any other cause of dementia, as this has implications for treatment approaches. If an adult with Prader-Willi syndrome develops psychosis, is this an organic disorder due to the Prader-Willi syndrome? Such a presumption cannot be made, in view of the many other possible aetiological factors, some of which are unknown. For example, presumably depression with psychotic features and schizophrenic/delusional episodes can sometimes occur in adults with Prader-Willi syndrome in a way that is *unrelated* to the Prader-Willi syndrome, in the same way that they can occur in the general population. Prader-Willi syndrome cannot be proven as the *cause* of the adult's psychosis in any individual case, and so should *not* be assumed, and the label 'organic' should be avoided. This individual approach differs from population approaches. In population approaches, if a higher rate of psychosis is demonstrated in a group with Prader-Willi syndrome compared with a matched control group of people with learning disabilities of other causes, the assumption can be made that Prader-Willi syndrome is associated with higher rates of psychosis. Even so, this does not prove an organic cause for the association, as psychological, social and developmental factors may be relevant and operate as modifying variables.

With regard to behavioural phenotypes, it is advisable to distinguish between 'additional disorders', and those disorders that are an integral part of the syndrome (i.e. a required clinical feature in order to diagnose the syndrome). For example, although dementia is common in middle-aged/ older adults with Down's syndrome, it does not occur in all, and is not a requirement in order to make the diagnosis of Down's syndrome. Therefore, dementia is an additional disorder that should be recorded as such. Over-eating is one of the clinical features listed in the diagnostic criteria for a clinical diagnosis of Prader-Willi syndrome (Holm *et al*, 1993). As such, the prevailing clinical wisdom is that it is an essential, integral part of Prader-Willi syndrome, rather than an 'additional disorder'. As over-eating is a clinical requirement to diagnose Prader-Willi syndrome, it would be inappropriate to count it twice by then diagnosing an additional eating disorder. Consequently for an adult with Prader-Willi syndrome, a diagnosis of an eating disorder would only be appropriate if there was a further comorbid condition, for example psychogenic vomiting disorder. Psychosis is not a clinical feature forming part of the diagnostic criteria for Prader-Willi syndrome, and so when it occurs it should be recorded as an additional psychiatric disorder.

This approach recognises the limitations of our existing knowledge. Down's syndrome is confirmed by genetic testing, and so the diagnosis can be made regardless of a person's clinical features. Although genetic testing is available for Prader-Willi syndrome, this is not yet routinely available in all countries, and the tests themselves are being further developed. Where genetic testing is not yet available, the diagnosis is therefore at present essentially a clinical diagnosis. For some syndromes of presumed genetic origin, the genetic lesion has yet to be identified, and no test is available, rendering the diagnosis solely a clinical one. Where this is the case, any clinical features required to diagnose the syndrome cannot be counted again as additional disorders.

As accurate genetic testing becomes available, it will be possible to move forward from this position, and probably discover that the severity/extent of any clinical feature will be normally distributed among all people with the syndrome. Some of the clinical features in existing diagnostic criteria for a syndrome may be recognised to only occur in a minority of individuals, whereas others may feature in all cases. Again, these are issues for future research when definitive diagnosis becomes available. However, we currently have to operate within the existing knowledge-base.

ICD–10 F06 and F07 should *not* be used for psychiatric presentations that are known to be associated with the adult's learning disabilities syndrome (behavioural phenotypes). Instead, the descriptive psychopathology within the psychiatric presentation should be used to diagnose an additional psychiatric disorder from categories within the ICD–10 manual, other than ICD–10 F06 or F07, or a category within DC–LD should be used.

A hierarchical approach to diagnosis

A hierarchical approach is adopted through and within axes:

- Axis I: Severity of learning disabilities
- Axis II: Cause of learning disabilities
- Axis III: Psychiatric disorders
  DC–LD Level A: Developmental disorders
  DC–LD Level B: Psychiatric illness
  DC–LD Level C: Personality disorders
  DC–LD Level D: Problem behaviours
  DC–LD Level E: Other disorders

The working group has focused on the development of Axes III DC–LD Levels B–D. Developmental disorders have been listed as a separate level in view of the recognition that the developmental disorder may not be the underlying cause of the person's learning disabilities (Axis II); for example, pervasive developmental disorders may coexist with syndromes such as Fragile X syndrome and Down's syndrome, and are not invariably associated with learning disabilities. Additionally, developmental disorders are distinct from psychiatric illnesses, although people with developmental disorders can develop comorbid Axis III DC–LD Levels B–D disorders.

The following case example illustrates the hierarchical approach to diagnosis. An adult with learning disabilities has excessive over-eating:

- *Axis I*
  Ascertain the adult's severity of learning disabilities. This does not, however, account for the person's excessive over-eating.

- *Axis II*
  Ascertain the adult's cause of his or her learning disabilities. If the adult has Prader-Willi syndrome then his or her excessive over-eating is a feature of this Axis II disorder. Alternatively, if the cause of the adult's learning disabilities is unknown or if it is a syndrome that does not rely upon the presence of excessive over-eating for its diagnosis, further Axes must be considered to account for the excessive over-eating.

- *Axis III: DC–LD Level A*
  Ascertain if the adult has a developmental disorder in addition to any Axis II disorders identified. If the excessive over-eating has not been accounted for by an Axis II disorder, is it solely due to a ritual forming part of a pervasive developmental disorder, if the person has such a disorder? As such, it may be explained by the DC–LD Level A disorder. However, if the excessive over-eating is not so explained, then proceed through the hierarchy.

Axis III: DC–LD Level B
If the excessive over-eating is not explained by any Axes II or III Level A disorders, ascertain if the symptom can be accounted for by any of the disorders in Axis III DC–LD Level B, for example depressive episode or a diagnosable eating disorder. Also, record if any other Axis III Level B disorders coexist.

Axis III: DC–LD Level C
Ascertain if there are features present to meet the criteria for a personality disorder. If so, is the excessive over-eating in keeping with the personality disorder? Proceed to DC–LD Level D if not.

Axis III: DC–LD Level D
If the over-eating has not yet been diagnosed, is it of sufficient severity, duration or frequency to meet criteria for a problem behaviour? Whether or not the person has

an Axis II or III Levels A–C disorder that accounts for the excessive over-eating, they may have other additional Axis III Level D problem behaviours that should be recorded.

Axis III: DC–LD Level E
Are any other disorders listed in Axis III DC–LD Level E present?

Using this approach, a symptom may sometimes be counted twice, if there are two different presentations of the same symptom. For example, an adult may have long-standing self-injurious behaviour – an Axis III Level D problem behaviour. If they develop a depressive episode (an Axis III Level B disorder), one of the symptoms within this disorder may be an increase in the person's severity/frequency of self-injurious behaviour over and above that which is usual for the person. (Of course, other symptoms of depressive episode would also have to be present in order to reach this diagnosis.) The person would receive a diagnosis on both Axis III Level B and Axis III Level D. Conversely, if the person only experiences self-injurious behaviour at the time of a depressive episode, and not at other times, he or she would receive a diagnosis on Axis III Level B only. Alternatively, the psychiatrist has the option to employ the supplementary criteria for problem behaviours that are a direct cause of other disorders, that is, 'problem behaviours due to psychiatric disorder (self-injurious behaviour)'. These optional supplementary criteria are only available in DC–LD Level D, and are not contained within other levels.

A further case example might be an adult with pervasive developmental disorder who has obsessional symptoms and anxiety symptoms (related to the obsessional symptoms). The pervasive developmental disorder would be recorded on Axis III Level A. A separate Axis III Level B diagnosis of obsessive–compulsive disorder would only be recorded if the adult met diagnostic criteria for obsessive–compulsive disorder, with symptoms over and above the baseline obsessions forming part of his or her pervasive develop-mental disorder. An exacerbation of obsessional symptoms in this adult might also be due to onset of other Axis III Level B disorders such as depressive episode: a full psychiatric assessment would be essential to delineate this.

In addition to a hierarchical approach to diagnosis through Axes and Levels, the hierarchical approach to diagnosis is also required within Levels. For example, obsessional symptoms may occur as part of a depressive episode: in this case, a separate diagnosis of obsessive–compulsive disorder would be inappropriate. There are many such examples, for example:

- Obsessional symptoms may be due to obsessive–compulsive disorder, or may be secondary to dementia, schizophrenic/delusional episode or depressive episode.

- Anxiety symptoms may be due to generalised anxiety disorder and panic disorder, or may be secondary to dementia, delirium, schizophrenic/delusional episode, depressive episode, phobic disorders or obsessive–compulsive disorder.

- Psychotic symptoms may be due to schizophrenic/delusional episodes and schizoaffective episode, but may be secondary to dementia, delirium, depressive episode, manic episode or mixed affective episode.

- Schizoaffective episode takes hierarchical precedence over schizophrenic/delusional episode, depressive episode, manic episode and mixed affective episode.

- Mixed affective episode takes hierarchical precedence over depressive episode and manic episode.

In these situations, the primary Axis III Level B disorder should be recorded. Careful and accurate history-taking is essential. Occasionally more than one Axis III Level B disorder may coexist.

The flow-chart in Fig. 5 outlines diagramatically the hierarchical approach to diagnosis that DC–LD adopts.

All of the Axes and Levels do not always need to be employed for an individual, although for some individuals all are required. Examples of how the described approach to psychiatric diagnosis can be used include the following brief case descriptions:

- Ms Susan Smith is a 37-year-old woman with severe learning disabilities (Axis I) due to Down's syndrome (Axis II) who has a six-month history of obsessive–compulsive disorder (Axis III Level B) and long-standing self-injurious behaviour through head-banging (Axis III Level D).

- Mr Rajesh Sharma is a 62-year-old-man with moderate learning disabilities (Axis I) of unknown cause (Axis II) who has a 20-year history of schizophrenic/delusional episode (Axis III Level B) and a two-year history of dementia (Axis III Level B).

- Mr Peter Jones is a 25-year-old man with severe learning disabilities (Axis I) and autism (Axis III Level A) who has a three-month history of depressive episode (Axis III Level B), long-standing pica (Axis III Level B), and long-standing self-injurious behaviour (Axis III Level D).

- Ms Josephine Bloggs is a 30-year-old woman with mild learning disabilities (Axis I) and tuberous sclerosis (Axis II) who has no additional Axis III disorders or behaviours.

- Mr Donald Allen is a 42-year-old man with moderate learning disabilities (Axis I) of unknown cause (Axis II), long-standing generalised anxiety disorder (Axis III Level B) and an anankastic personality (Axis III Level C).

These case descriptions are clearly very brief. Including additional information (e.g. severity and frequency of Axis III Level D problem behaviours and the types of clinical management/interventions/supports that are needed) would be helpful in clinical summaries, as would providing information on aetiology of disorders and problem behaviours, and on associated physical disorders/disabilities.

AXIS I: SEVERITY OF LEARNING DISABILITIES

Severity of learning disabilities: Introduction

These disorders include:

- Mild learning disabilities [F70. *x*]; [317]
  IQ range = 50–69; mental age = 9 to under 12 years.
- Moderate learning disabilities [F71. *x*]; [318.0]
  IQ range = 35–49; mental age = 6 to under 9 years.
- Severe learning disabilities [F72. *x*]; [318.1]
  IQ range = 20–34; mental age = 3 to under 6 years.
- Profound learning disabilities [F73. *x*]; [318.2]
  IQ range <20; mental age = <3 years.
- Other learning disabilities [F78. *x*]; [–]
- Unspecified learning disabilities [F79. *x*]; [319]

The ICD–10 manuals use the term 'mental retardation'. DC–LD has adopted the term 'learning disabilities': this is used synonymously with the ICD–10 term mental retardation. The diagnosis of mental retardation is dependent upon the person having an intelligence quotient below 70, together with continued impairment in adaptive behaviour/social functioning, and with onset during the developmental phase (i.e. before the age of 18 years). The term 'borderline learning disabilities' is not included in ICD–10, and nor is it included in DC–LD. It is unlikely that people functioning above the mild learning disabilities range would require the use of the diagnostic criteria within DC–LD: indeed, this is also true for many people with mild learning disabilities, for whom ICD–10 criteria may be more appropriate. Within most European and North American cultures, ICD–10 recommends the use of the Vineland Adaptive Behaviour Scales (Sparrow *et al*, 1984) as an assessment tool.

ICD–10 allows additional sub-classification of codes F70–79 to record the presence or absence of impairment of behaviour. This is contrary to the approach taken by DC–LD, and DC–LD recommends that such sub-classification is not employed.

For further information and diagnostic criteria regarding ICD–10 F70–F79 codes, the ICD–10 manuals should be consulted.

AXIS II: CAUSES OF LEARNING DISABILITIES

Causes of learning disabilities: Introduction

These disorders include the following (listed in ICD–10 chapter order):

- II 1.1   Unknown

Chapter I: Certain infectious and parasitic diseases

- Meningococcal meningitis [A39.0]
- Other meningococcal infections [A39.8]
  Includes meningococcal encephalitis.
- Congenital syphilis, unspecified [A50.9]
- Slow virus infection of the central nervous system [A81]
- Herpes virus encephalitis [B00.4]
- Measles complicated by encephalitis [B05.0]

Chapter IV: Endocrine, nutritional and metabolic diseases

- Congenital iodine-deficiency syndrome, unspecified [E00.9]
- Hypofunction and other disorders of pituitary gland [E23]
- Phenylketonuria [E70.0]
- Maple-syrup-urine disease [E71.0]
- Other disorders of branch-chain amino-acid metabolism [E71.1]
  Includes hypervalinaemia; methylmalonic acidaemia.
- Disorders of amino-acid transport [E72.0]
  Includes Hartnup disease.
- Disorders of sulphur-bearing amino-acid metabolism [E72.1]
  Includes homocystinuria.
- Disorder of amino-acid metabolism, unspecified [E72.9]
- GM_2 gangliosidosis [E75.0]
  Includes Tay-Sachs disease; Sandhoff disease.
- Other sphingolipidoses [E75.2]
  Includes Gaucher syndrome; Niemann-Pick syndrome.

- Mucopolysaccharidosis, type I [E76.0]
  Includes Hurler syndrome.
- Mucopolysaccharidosis, type II [E76.1]
  Includes Hunter syndrome.
- Other mucopolysaccharidoses [E76.2]
  Includes Sanfilippo (type B; type C; type D) syndrome.
- Lesch-Nyhan syndrome [E79.1]
- Disorders of copper metabolism [E83.0]
  Includes Menkes' kinky hair disease; Wilson's disease.

Chapter V: Mental and behavioural disorders

- Rett syndrome [F84.2]; [equivalent to 299.80]

Chapter VI: Diseases of the nervous system

- Bacterial meningitis, unspecified [G00.9]
- Acute disseminated encephalitis [G04.0]
  Includes post-immunisation encephalitis; post-immunisation encephalomyelitis.
- Encephalitis, myelitis and encephalomyelitis, unspecified [G04.9]

Chapter XVI: Certain conditions originating in the perinatal period

- Foetus and newborn affected by unspecified maternal condition [P00.9]
  Includes maternal hypertension; maternal infectious and parasitic diseases; maternal nutritional disorders; radiology on mother.
- Foetus and newborn affected by maternal complications of pregnancy, unspecified [P01.9]
- Foetus and newborn affected by placenta praevia [P02.0]
- Foetus and newborn affected by other forms of placental separation and haemorrhage [P02.1]
  Includes abruptio placentae; antepartum haemorrhage.
- Foetus and newborn affected by other and unspecified morphological and functional abnormalities of placenta [P02.2]
  Includes placental dysfunction; placental infarction; placental insufficiency.
- Foetus and newborn affected by other and unspecified conditions of umbilical cord [P02.6]
  Includes prolapsed cord; other cord compression; vasa praevia.

- Foetus and newborn affected by complications of labour and delivery, unspecified [P03.9]
  Includes precipitant delivery; malpresentation.
- Foetus and newborn affected by maternal noxious influences, unspecified [P04.9]
  Includes maternal use of drugs of addiction and alcohol (but *excludes* foetal alcohol syndrome); maternal exposure to environmental chemical substances; maternal medication with cytotoxic drugs.
- Extremely low birth weight [P07.0]
  Birth weight 999g or less.
- Extreme immaturity [P07.2]
  Less than 28 complete weeks (196 complete days) of gestation.
- Unspecified intracranial laceration and haemorrhage due to birth injury [P10.9]
- Birth injury to central nervous system, unspecified [P11.9]
- Intrauterine hypoxia, unspecified [P20.9]
- Birth asphyxia, unspecified [P21.9]
- Congenital rubella syndrome [P35.0]
- Congenital cytomegalovirus syndrome [P35.1]
- Congenital viral disease, unspecified [P35.9]
- Bacterial sepsis of newborn, unspecified [P36.9]
- Congenital toxoplasmosis [P37.1]
- Neonatal listeriosis [P37.2]
- Congenital infectious or parasitic disease, unspecified [P37.9]
- Intracranial (non-traumatic) haemorrhage of foetus and newborn, unspecified [P52.9]
  Includes intracranial haemorrhage due to anoxia or hypoxia.
- Haemorrhagic disease of foetus and newborn [P53]
- Rhesus isoimmunization of foetus and newborn [P55.0]
- ABO isoimmunization of foetus and newborn [P55.1]
- Kernicterus, unspecified [P57.9]

Chapter XVII: Congenital malformations, deformities, and chromosomal abnormalities

- Encephalocele, unspecified [Q01.9]
- Microcephaly [Q02]
- Congenital hydrocephalus, unspecified [Q03.9]
- Congenital malformation of corpus callosum [Q04.0]
- Congenital malformation of brain, unspecified [Q04.9]
- Arnold-Chiari syndrome [Q07.0]

- Neurofibromatosis [Q85.0]
- Tuberous sclerosis [Q85.1]
- Other phakomatoses, not elsewhere classified [Q85.1]
  Includes Sturge-Weber syndrome.
- Foetal alcohol syndrome [Q86.0]
- Congenital malformation syndromes predominantly
  affecting facial appearance [Q87.0]
  Includes Apert syndrome; Treacher Collins syndrome.
- Congenital malformation syndromes predominantly
  associated with short stature [Q87.1]
  Includes Aaskog syndrome; Prader-Willi syndrome; de
  Lange syndrome; Noonan syndrome; Seckel syndrome;
  Smith-Lemli-Opitz syndrome; Aicardi syndrome.
- Congenital malformation syndromes predominantly
  involving limbs [Q87.2]
  Includes Rubenstein-Taybi syndrome.
- Congenital malformation syndromes involving early
  overgrowth [Q87.3]
  Includes Sotos syndrome.
- Other specified congenital malformation syndromes, not
  elsewhere classified [Q87.8]
  Includes Lawrence-Moon-Biedl syndrome; Zellweger
  syndrome.
- Down's syndrome
  - ➤ Trisomy 21, meiotic non-dysjunction [Q90.0]
  - ➤ Trisomy 21, mosaicism [Q90.1]
  - ➤ Trisomy 21, translocation [Q90.2]
  - ➤ Down's syndrome, unspecified [Q90.9]
- Edward's syndrome, unspecified [Q91.3]
- Patau's syndrome, unspecified [Q91.7]
- Trisomy and partial trisomy of autosomes, unspecified [Q92]
- Deletion of short arm of chromosome 5 (Cri du Chat
  syndrome) [Q93.4]
- Deletion from autosomes, unspecified [Q93.9]
  Includes Angelman syndrome; Smith-Magenis syndrome;
  Velocardiofacial syndrome; Williams syndrome.
- Turner syndrome, unspecified [Q96.9]
- Sex chromosome abnormality, female phenotype,
  unspecified [Q97.9]
- Klinefelter syndrome, unspecified [Q98.4]
- Sex chromosome abnormality, male phenotype,
  unspecified [Q98.9]
- Fragile X syndrome [Q99.2]
- Chromosomal abnormality, unspecified [Q99.9]

Chapter XIX: Injury, poisoning and certain other consequences of external cause

* Intracranial injury, unspecified [S06.9]

Axis II refers to the cause of the person's learning disabilities. Those users who wish to consult a list of other medical conditions that a person may have (e.g. epilepsy), but which are not aetiological to the person's learning disabilities, should refer to Appendix 2. There are many possible causes of learning disabilities coded in the ICD–10 manuals. The list above includes examples taken from the manuals. The ICD–10 manuals should be consulted for a more extensive list, and for diagnostic criteria. Note that ICD–10 includes Rett syndrome as a pervasive developmental disorder, while acknowledging the uncertainties regarding the nosological status of some categories of pervasive developmental disorder. DC–LD includes Rett syndrome as a genetic cause of learning disabilities. Cerebral palsy has been listed in Appendix 2 (ICD–10 chapters other than V – Other associated medical conditions) rather than in Axis II.

AXIS III: PSYCHIATRIC DISORDERS

DC–LD LEVEL A: DEVELOPMENTAL DISORDERS

Pervasive developmental disorders: Introduction

These disorders include:

- IIIA1.1 Autism (childhood onset) [equivalent to F84.0]; [equivalent to 299.00]
- IIIA1.2 Autism (age of onset unknown) [equivalent to F84.0]; [equivalent to 299.00]
- Other ICD–10 pervasive developmental disorders

DC–LD has not modified the diagnostic criteria for the ICD–10 pervasive developmental disorders. However, terminology has been changed from 'childhood autism' to 'autism (childhood onset)', as this was felt to be more appropriate for an adult population. The criteria within this category have not been changed from ICD–10. A new category has been introduced: 'autism (age of onset unknown)'. This is in recognition of the lack of available developmental histories for some adults with learning disabilities who otherwise have the core features of autism. For further information regarding the ICD–10 F84.0 codes and diagnostic criteria, the ICD–10 manuals should be consulted.

Contrary to the approach adopted in the ICD–10 manuals, Rett syndrome is viewed as distinct from the pervasive developmental disorders. Consequently, it has been excluded from Axis III DC–LD Level A, and is listed instead on Axis II.

IIIA1.1 Autism (childhood onset)

A The ICD–10 criteria for childhood autism are met.

IIIA1.2 Autism (age of onset unknown)

A The age of onset of the disorder is unknown, owing to lack of any available written early developmental history and lack of any possible informant history regarding early development. However, the disorder is known to be long-standing, extending back as far as the available history.

B Other ICD–10 criteria for childhood autism are met.

Other ICD–10 pervasive developmental disorders

ICD–10 also includes other pervasive developmental disorders. The ICD–10 manuals should be consulted for details of diagnostic criteria if use of these categories is considered:

- Atypical autism
  - ➢ Atypicality in symptomatology [F84.11]; [equivalent to 299.80]
  - ➢ Atypicality in both age of onset and symptomatology [F84.12]; [equivalent to 299.80]
- Other childhood disintegrative disorders [F84.3]; [equivalent to 299.10]
- Overactive disorder associated with mental retardation and stereotyped movements [F84.4]; [equivalent to 307.3]
- Asperger's syndrome [F84.5]; [equivalent to 299.80]
- Other pervasive developmental disorders [F84.8]; [equivalent to 299.80]
- Pervasive developmental disorder, unspecified [F84.9]; [–]

Specific developmental disorders: Introduction

ICD–10 also includes a number of specific developmental disorders. The ICD–10 manuals should be consulted for details of diagnostic criteria if use of these categories is considered:

- Specific developmental disorder of speech and language
  - ➢ Specific speech articulation disorder [F80.0]; [equivalent to 315.39]
  - ➢ Expressive language disorder [F80.1]; [equivalent to 315.31]
  - ➢ Receptive language disorder [F80.2]; [equivalent to 315.31]
  - ➢ Acquired aphasia with epilepsy (Landau-Kleffner syndrome) [F80.3]; [–]
  - ➢ Other developmental disorders of speech and language [F80.8]; [equivalent to 307.9]
- Specific developmental disorder of scholastic skills
  - ➢ Specific reading disorder [F81.0]; [equivalent to 315.00]
  - ➢ Specific spelling disorder [F81.1]; [–]
  - ➢ Specific disorder of arithmetical skills [F81.2]; [equivalent to 315.1]
  - ➢ Mixed disorder of scholastic skills [F81.3]; [–]
  - ➢ Other developmental disorders of scholastic skills [F81.8]; [equivalent to 315.9]

**Axis III
DC-LD Level A**

- Specific developmental disorder of motor function [F82]; [equivalent to 315.4]
- Mixed specific developmental disorders [F83]; [–]
- Disorders of written expression [–]; [equivalent to 315.2]
- Stuttering [F98.5]; [equivalent to 307.0]
- Cluttering [F98.6]; [–]

DC–LD LEVEL B: PSYCHIATRIC ILLNESS

Dementia: Introduction

DC–LD includes the following disorders in this group:

- IIIB1.1   Unspecified dementia [equivalent to F03]; [equivalent to 294.8]
- IIIB1.2   Dementia in Alzheimer's disease, unspecified [equivalent to F00.9*xx*]; [equivalent to 290.0, 290.1*x*, 290.2*x*, 290.3]
- IIIB1.3   Vascular dementia, unspecified [equivalent to F01.9*xx*]; [equivalent to 290.4*x*]
- IIIB1.4   Dementia in Huntington's disease [equivalent to F02.2*xx*]; [equivalent to 294.1]
- Other ICD–10 dementias

The stages in the process to diagnose dementia are no different to those of diagnosis of other psychiatric disorders. It requires accurate determination of the presenting psycho-pathology and its duration. This requires distinguishing between how the person is now, compared with how they were in the past. As for all psychiatric disorders, it is dependent upon accurate informant history – in the absence of this, a diagnosis is difficult to make. It is worth noting the following diagnostic points:

- It is not possible to diagnose dementia on the basis of a single psychometric examination of the person.

- It is not possible to diagnose dementia on the basis of repeat psychometric examination or repeat adaptive behaviour skills assessment of the person alone – as a decline on such assessments has many possible causes. However, such assessments may be used in conjunction with the psychiatric and physical assessments that are always required, and may be useful in monitoring the progression of the disorder.

- As for other psychiatric disorders, if there is a good informant who has known the person with learning disabilities for a number of years, dementia can be diagnosed at a single psychiatric assessment. This is provided that:

  1 the assessment excludes other psychiatric and physical factors as the cause of the presentation, that is, a full psychiatric and physical assessment is undertaken; and

  2 clear examples are given in all categories of how the person presents/functions now and how on the same item they used to present/function in the past. There must be definite evidence of change having occurred across several items. Clear examples are required in each case; a general impression of decline or change is inadequate.

- A six-month or longer history is useful to distinguish dementia from delirium.

- Although onset of, or increase in, aphasia, apraxia and agnosia are recognised features of dementia in the general population, these have not been included in DC–LD. This is because of the difficulty in measuring such symptoms in people with learning disabilities, particularly when assessing change in symptoms from baseline functioning. However, where these symptoms can be identified, they may be considered as additional findings supportive of a diagnosis of dementia. Other neurological symptoms, such as the onset of seizures and frontal lobe release signs, while not part of the core psychopathology of dementia, are also additional findings supportive to the diagnosis of dementia.

Within the general population, dementia is sometimes subdivided into mild, moderate and severe subtypes. Within the boundaries of the existing knowledge base, it is difficult to be prescriptive as to how such subdivisions may be made in people with learning disabilities. In many cases, it is more appropriate to make a diagnosis of 'dementia', rather than commenting on severity. Clinical experience may be helpful to stage dementia in individual cases.

Among the general population, it is usual to subdivide dementia into different subtypes; for example, dementia in Alzheimer's disease, vascular dementia, Lewy body dementia, dementia in Huntington's disease, dementia in Pick's disease and dementia in Creutzfeldt-Jakob's disease. It is likely that these differing subtypes of dementia all occur in people with learning disabilities. However, the diagnostic challenge in sub-classifying, which at times is difficult with members of the general population, is greater when working with people with learning disabilities. Consequently, where any doubt as to subtype exists, unspecified dementia is the recommended category, as this can be diagnosed with some certainty. When sub-classification is undertaken further than this, it is not recommended to include subtypes other than dementia in Alzheimer's disease, vascular dementia or dementia in Huntington's disease. DC–LD criteria for these disorders are included. It should be acknowledged that even limited sub-classification beyond unspecified dementia may be associated with error and the definitive diagnosis depends on post-mortem neuropathology. Sometimes, dementia subtypes can coexist (e.g. mixed vascular dementia/dementia in Alzheimer's disease), presenting even greater difficulty in diagnostic sub-classification.

Criteria are listed below for unspecified dementia, which is the recommended diagnostic category for most cases. These criteria must be met before sub-classification into dementia subtypes. Additional clinical findings that may be supportive in distinguishing between dementia in Alzheimer's disease and vascular dementia include the nature of onset and course of progression of the dementia, variability in the person's presentation, presence or absence of associated focal signs, episodes of impaired consciousness, hypertension, extent of insight, emotional lability and personality changes. Some of the distinguishing features are included on the Hachinski scale (Hachinski *et al*, 1975), but skill, training and care is required in its interpretation when used with people with learning disabilities.

Although other psychiatric and physical disorders can coexist with dementia, it is important to exclude them as the primary cause of the person's dementia. When uncertainty exists, the diagnosis of dementia should not be made. Depression can occur in a person with dementia and should be treated along standard lines for depression. When a person presents for the first time with symptoms of both depression and dementia, even when a good informant who has known the person for a number of years is available, it may be difficult to clarify the history with certainty. In such cases, there should be a trial of treatment for depression, rather than a diagnosis of dementia, with diagnosis being delayed. The nature of the person's disorder(s) may become clearer with the passage of time.

Non-cognitive symptoms (e.g. depressive symptoms and psychotic symptoms) are recognised to be an integral part of dementia both in the general population and in people with learning disabilities. The diagnostic issue is to distinguish symptoms from syndromes; for example, labile mood in the absence of other depressive symptoms would not warrant a diagnosis of depression and can be assumed to be a non-cognitive symptom of dementia. Conversely, where several depressive symptoms coexist, these warrant a clinical trial of antidepressant treatment, even if full diagnostic criteria for depression have not been met.

IIIB1.1   Unspecified dementia

A   The symptoms/signs must be present for **at least a six-month duration**. A shorter duration may point towards a tentative diagnosis, whereas the six-month duration leads to a more confident diagnosis.

B   They must not be a direct consequence of other psychiatric or physical disorders. Although other psychiatric disorders may coexist with dementia, they should be excluded as the primary cause of the 'dementia' symptoms, for example apparent cognitive decline as a symptom of depression.

C   The symptoms/signs must represent a change from the person's premorbid state. Specific examples must be given to demonstrate change in each category, that is, things that the person used to be able to do but is now no longer able to. A general impression of deterioration is not adequate to meet this item.

D   Impaired memory must be present. Examples include: getting muddled and confused when this was not previously the case for the person; forgetting where items have been placed or social/work events that have been attended when such information would characteristically have been remembered in the past; forgetting simple information the person has just been told; forgetting names of people that he or she used to know and use; getting lost in places that were previously familiar and which the person could find his or her way around; being unable to follow instructions that he or she would previously have found easy to follow (or requiring instructions to be broken down into simpler/fewer steps in order to complete tasks); no longer recognising familiar people who were previously always recognised.

E   Impairment of other cognitive skills, judgement and thinking must be present. Examples include: loss of accuracy of language skills; mixing up day and night by a person who used to distinguish between these, for example getting up in the middle of the night insisting that it is time for work; loss of ability in reading or writing skills (this requires specific evidence of/examples of present compared with past skills); loss of ability to budget or count change or handle money (dependent on previous money skills level as above); loss of specific self-care skills, such as the ability to shampoo hair, washing, shaving, dressing, shopping, toileting, etc. Loss of skills includes being unable to do tasks that were previously completed and/or requiring more verbal prompts and reminders to complete tasks. In all cases specific evidence of/examples of present compared with past skills are required.

F   Items D and E above must not be solely attributed to clouding of consciousness as in delirium (i.e. the person must demonstrate clear consciousness).

G   Reduced emotional control or motivation or change in social behaviour must be present. Examples include: emotional lability; irritability; apathy; loss of self-direction/ motivation; reduced quantity of speech/social interaction; coarsening of existing personality traits.

If these criteria are satisfied and other psychiatric and physical disorders have been excluded as the cause of the symptoms, a general diagnosis of dementia can be made. There are many causes of dementia, and subtypes of dementia. Further differentiation of dementia is reliant upon medical interpretation of the course and pattern of the disorder, the symptom profile, and physical, laboratory and radiological examination.

IIIB1.2   Dementia in Alzheimer's disease, unspecified

A   The criteria for unspecified dementia are met.

B   There is no evidence from the history, physical examination, or special investigations for any other possible cause of dementia (e.g. cerebrovascular disease, Parkinson's disease, Huntington's disease, hypothyroidism, vitamin B12 or folic acid deficiency, hyper-calcaemia, alcohol or drug misuse).

IIIB1.3   Vascular dementia, unspecified

A   The criteria for unspecified dementia are met.

B   Some higher cognitive functions have been affected by the process to a greater extent than others, which may be relatively spared.

C   There is clinical evidence of the onset of focal brain damage by the presence of one of the following:
1   Onset of or increase in unilateral spastic weakness of the limbs
2   Onset of or increase in unilateral tendon hyper-reflexia
3   Onset of an extensor plantar response, where this has previously been documented to be flexor
4   Onset of pseudobulbar palsy.

D   There is evidence from the history, examination, or tests of a significant cerebro-vascular disease, which is judged to be aetiological to the dementia (e.g. a history of stroke; evidence of cerebral infarction).

**Axis III
DC–LD Level B**

IIIB1.4   Dementia in Huntington's disease

A   The criteria for unspecified dementia are met.

B   Choreiform movements are present (typically of the face, hands or shoulders, or in the gait), with onset in late childhood or adult life, and not accounted for by another disorder.

C   There is a family history of Huntington's disease, or suggestive of Huntington's disease.

Other ICD–10 dementias

Other types of dementia are included in ICD–10. The ICD–10 manuals should be consulted for details of diagnostic criteria if use of these categories is considered:

•   Dementia in Alzheimer's disease with early onset [F00.0*xx*]; [equivalent to 290.1*x*]

- Dementia in Alzheimer's disease with late onset [F00.1*xx*]; [equivalent to 290.0, 290.2*x*, 290.3]
- Dementia in Alzheimer's disease, atypical or mixed type [F00.2*xx*]; [equivalent to 290.0, 290.10]
- Vascular dementia of acute onset [F01.0*xx*]; [equivalent to 290.40]
- Multi-infarct dementia [F01.1*xx*]; [equivalent to 290.40]
- Sub-cortical vascular dementia [F01.2*xx*]; [equivalent to 290.40]
- Mixed cortical and subcortical vascular dementia [F01.3*xx*]; [equivalent to 290.40]
- Other vascular dementia [F01.9*xx*]; [equivalent to 290.40]
- Dementia in Pick's disease [F02.0*xx*]; [equivalent to 290.10]
- Dementia in Creutzfeldt-Jakob disease [F02.1*xx*]; [equivalent to 290.10]
- Dementia in Parkinson's disease [F02.3*xx*]; [equivalent to 294.1]
- Dementia in human immunodeficiency virus disease [F02.4*xx*]; [equivalent to 294.9]
- Dementia in other specified diseases classified elsewhere [F02.8*xx*]; [equivalent to 294.1]
- Organic amnesic syndrome, not induced by alcohol and other psychoactive substances [F04]; [equivalent to 294.0, 294.8]
- Dementia due to head trauma [F02.8]; [294.1]

Delirium: Introduction

This group of disorders have been collapsed into one DC–LD category:

- IIIB2.1   Delirium [equivalent to F05.*x*]; [equivalent to 293.0, 780.09]

Delirium (acute and sub-acute confusional states) occurs relatively commonly in adults with learning disabilities when compared with the general population, probably because pre-existing brain dysfunction acts as a predisposing factor. Such states may occur, for example, in acutely and chronically physically ill, ageing and physically frail adults. Delirium may also be superimposed on or progress to dementia. Delirium associated with alcohol or substance misuse is *not* included here, but instead should be classified in reference to ICD–10 categories F10–F19.

Causes of delirium, with acute or sub-acute onset include, for example, septicaemia, urinary, chest, central nervous system and other infections, and cancer, cardio-pulmonary, liver, renal, metabolic, autoimmune and other systemic physical health disorders. Delirium may also follow medication changes such as commencing new medications, and the development of medication toxicity, especially during anticonvulsant/psychotropic polytherapy. Sometimes the physical cause of the delirium cannot be determined, but thorough physical examination and investigation is always required, in addition to the psychiatric assessment.

When the adult with learning disabilities is obviously acutely physically unwell, the diagnostic features of delirium, if subtle, may be overlooked, given the understandable and necessary focus on his or her physical health treatment. However, delirium may also present with more overt features, such as the person exhibiting diurnally fluctuating severe confusion, and disturbed and uncooperative behaviours. Usually, onset of delirium is rapid and resolution occurs within weeks with the appropriate physical investigations, diagnosis and treatment of the underlying physical disorder. However, less dramatic sub-acute confusional states lasting up to six months (such as due to subdural haematoma or chronic medication toxicity) can also occur and are less likely to be appropriately diagnosed and treated. In these cases, a key diagnostic feature (as in more acute presentations) is that the symptoms constitute a change from the person's usual baseline pattern of functioning, cognition, emotional responses and behaviour. If previous baseline results are available, current physical examination findings, abnormalities on special investigations and abnormal slowing of background electroencephalogram (EEG) activity (compared with baseline) can provide supporting evidence of current cerebral dysfunction.

Further research is needed to establish the underlying causes, common clinical features, prevalence, appropriate prevention, clinical management approaches and outcomes of delirium in adults with learning disabilities.

IIIB2.1 Delirium

A   The symptoms/signs fluctuate in intensity within each 24-hour period, and may be transient. Their duration must be **less than six months.**

B   The symptoms/signs are not a direct consequence of alcohol or substance intoxication or withdrawal.

C   The symptoms/signs must represent a change from the person's premorbid pattern of functioning, cognition, and emotional and behavioural traits.

D   The symptoms/signs arise during the course of a diagnosed or *suspected* physical disorder.

E   Item 1 or 2 must be present:
    1   Fluctuating impairment of consciousness. This may include clouding of consciousness, drowsiness, sleep, coma, or an abnormal rate of transition between levels of wakefulness
    2   Reduction in ability to direct, focus, sustain and shift attention, compared with the person's usual ability.

F   One of the following must be present:
    1   Fluctuating visual and/or other perceptual hallucinations and/or illusions
    2   Reduced understanding, judgement and thinking compared with the person's usual ability; or transient secondary delusions
    3   Reduced short-term (immediate and recent) memory compared with the person's usual ability
    4   Fluctuating level of orientation.

G   Fluctuating psychomotor disturbances must be present. These may include underactivity, overactivity, or both, if these are unusual for the person; increased or reduced speech; increased startle response; increased reaction time or increased time to respond to prompts when compared with the person's usual ability.

H   Onset of or increased emotional disturbances must be present, for example, misery, lability, anxiety, fear, irritability, euphoria, apathy or perplexity.

I   Onset of or increased disturbance of sleep–wake cycle must be present. This may include the onset of or increase in insomnia, reversed sleep–wake cycle, daytime drowsiness, nightmares, and/or nocturnal worsening of symptoms listed in E–H above.

Non-affective psychotic disorders: Introduction

DC–LD includes the following disorders in this group:

- IIIB3.1*x*   Schizophrenic/delusional episode; schizophrenic/delusional disorders [equivalent to F20. *xx*, F22. *x*, F23. *xx*]; [equivalent to 295. *xx*, 295.40, 297.1, 298.8]
- IIIB3.2*xx*   Schizoaffective episode; schizoaffective disorders [equivalent to F25. *xx*]; [equivalent to 295.70]
- IIIB3.3   Other non-affective psychotic disorders [equivalent to F28]; [equivalent to 298.9]
- Other ICD–10 non-affective psychotic disorders

Non-affective psychotic disorders occur more commonly in adults with learning disabilities than in other adults. This is in spite of the diagnostic difficulty presented by people with limited verbal communication skills, and the impossibility at present of diagnosing non-affective psychotic disorders in adults without communication skills. It is unlikely that schizophrenic/delusional episodes could be diagnosed in most adults with profound learning disabilities. This results in a proportion of such disorders being undetected, since a neurodevelopmental/genetic/brain trauma aetiological model for schizophrenia would imply occurrence in a proportion of people with all severities of learning disabilities, including those recorded on Axis I to have profound learning disabilities.

In view of the limitations in eliciting psychopathology for this group of disorders in adults with learning disabilities, it is not usually appropriate or valid to sub-classify the disorders to the extent described in the ICD–10 manuals. The terms schizophrenic/delusional episode and disorders are used in DC–LD as all-embracing terms to include a range of subtypes in ICD–10, including the schizophrenias, persistent delusional disorders, acute and transient psychotic disorders and persistent hallucinatory disorders. Psychotic disorders occurring as part of a primary affective disorder, dementia or delirium are specifically excluded from this category; their primary Axis III Level B diagnostic category should be recorded instead. However, it should be noted that conditions can occur comorbidly: a person with long-standing schizophrenic/delusional disorder may subsequently develop a depressive episode or dementia.

Axis III
DC–LD Level B

The quality of psychotic symptoms within these disorders differs from those seen in the general population. Within the general population, delusions are said to be false beliefs that are held to a firm, unshakeable extent. People with learning disabilities frequently give compliant answers, especially when pressurised to do so. Consequently, it is possible to talk a person with learning disabilities 'out of' the delusional belief, in much the same way that the person can be persuaded to give false answers or compliant answers to other questions or allegations. A better indicator of delusions therefore is when the false belief is repeatedly stated; for example, the person may be talked out of the belief, but almost immediately afterwards reiterates it voluntarily, or when asked. It is particularly important that interviewers pay attention to this issue when eliciting psychopathology, and as far as possible ask 'open' and non-leading questions. Similarly a person with learning disabilities may report auditory hallucinations, but might be temporarily persuaded to agree that they are not real, or that they are mistaken. Almost immediately afterwards, they revert to the original claim. It is always important, however, to distinguish delusions and hallucinations from simple misunderstandings or from fantasies.

Whereas delusions and hallucinations in a fully awake person are always abnormal findings in terms of the form of the psychopathology (and so indicate psychiatric illness), their content is often developmentally appropriate for the person's overall ability level. Examples include delusions about witches, monsters, ghosts and pop stars. Where an adult's life experiences have been within infantilising contexts, the content of hallucinations may reflect this, such as accusations or imperative commands regarding 'naughtiness'. Such reports must be taken seriously as they indicate major psychiatric illness in this population.

Some 'positive' symptoms that are seen in the general population with schizophrenia are uncommon in people with learning disabilities. Examples include delusional perception, passivity phenomena, thought echo, hallucinatory voices giving a running commentary and thought alienation. This may relate more to the difficulty in eliciting such phenomena from people with limited verbal skills and intellect, rather than such symptoms not occurring. Other symptoms occurring in the general population with schizophrenia that are considered to have special diagnostic significance are also found in some people with learning disabilities who have psychotic disorders. Such examples include third-person auditory hallucinations, hallucinations emanating from some part of the body and impossible/fantastic delusions. Sometimes it is not possible to separate out third-person, second-person and elemental auditory hallucinations. Hallucinations may occur in all sensory modalities, for example, visual hallucinations may occur. Catatonic symptoms can occur, but, as in the general population with schizophrenia, are now an unusual feature of the disorder. Disorder of the form of thoughts (disconnection in sequence of thoughts) and neologisms can also occur, but diagnostic care must be taken to distinguish such symptoms from normal developmental findings for the person; that is, a clear history of change is required, with good background history regarding the person's previous linguistic developmental level.

'Negative' symptoms that feature within the general population with schizophrenia are also found within adults with learning disabilities and non-affective psychotic disorders. However, for some individuals with a long history over many years, there are sometimes difficulties in determining premorbid levels of social functioning and skills. For some individuals there is a pattern of continuing deterioration of such symptoms, or an alternating pattern of deterioration and recovery. However, a proportion of people with learning disabilities and non-affective psychotic disorders experience episodes characterised by delusions and hallucinations, which respond well to treatment and have relative preservation of personality, skills and motivational level between and within episodes.

Sometimes non-affective psychotic disorders first present as a change in the person's behaviour, or by the person behaving in an odd, bizarre or uncharacteristic way, or with an increase in or onset of verbal or physical aggression to people or property, or by the person becoming socially withdrawn and seemingly speaking to themselves or to another person when no one appears to be there, or by the person pointing to things, picking or swiping at things that others cannot see. In such cases (as all of these findings may, or equally may not, be due to a psychotic disorder), a comprehensive psychiatric assessment should be undertaken. Attempts to elicit psychopathology that might account for the above findings should be made by 'open' questioning, followed by progressively more direct questions to prompt discussion.

Prompts covering the following areas are recommended:

1   Has anything new happened to the person?
2   Does he or she have any new ideas?
3   Has he or she found out anything new or special or strange?
4   Has anyone been getting at him or her?
5   Has anyone been picking on him or her?
6   Is anyone against him or her?
7   Is anyone trying to harm him or her?
8   Has anything special happened?
9   Has the television/radio been troubling him or her?
10 Has there been anything special on the television/radio?
11 Has he or she received any special messages?
12 Has he or she been on the television?
13 Has anyone been talking behind his or her back?
14 Has anyone been saying bad things to him or her?
15 Has anyone been telling him or her to do bad things?
16 Has he or she heard someone speaking when there is no one in the room?
17 Has he or she seen anything frightening?
18 Has he or she seen things other people say are not there?
19 Has anyone been interfering with him or her?

All of these prompts require further expansion and clarification, dependent upon the person's reply, such as asking for a description of the last time it happened, as all may elicit descriptions of normal events and experiences, as well as psychotic psychopathology. Considerable care, experience and special training are required to undertake such an interview/assessment.

Non-affective psychotic disorders occur more commonly in people with a history of such disorders in first- and second-degree relatives.

IIIB3.1*x*   Schizophrenic/delusional episode

A   The symptoms/signs must not be a direct consequence of other psychiatric disorders (e.g. dementia, delirium, depressive episode, manic episode, mixed affective episode), prescribed or illegal drugs or alcohol or physical disorders such as thyroid dysfunction.

B   The criteria for schizoaffective episode are not met. (Hierarchically, schizoaffective episode takes precedence over schizophrenic/delusional episode.)

C One of item groups 1, 2 *or* 3 must be present:

1 One of the following symptoms must be present **on most days for at least two weeks**:

   a Third-person auditory hallucinations (hallucinatory voices discussing the person among themselves)

   b Hallucinatory voices from some part of the body

   c Impossible/fantastic delusions (delusions are culturally inappropriate and completely impossible, for example, being able to communicate with aliens)

   d Thought insertion *or* withdrawal *or* broadcasting; *or* thought echo; *or* delusions of control, influence or passivity (clearly referred to body or limb movements or specific thoughts, actions or sensations); *or* delusional perception; *or* hallucinatory voices giving a running commentary.

2 One of the following symptoms is present for **most of the time during a one-month period, or some time every day for at least one-month** (a longer timescale, in view of the lesser diagnostic significance of these symptoms):

   a Delusions that are not mood congruent (delusions cannot be explained by the person's religious, cultural and environmental background)

   b Hallucinations that are not mood congruent – these may occur in any sensory modality.

3 Two of the following symptoms must be present **on most days for at least two weeks**, although may change in intensity and type from day to day:

   a Delusions, that are not mood congruent (delusions cannot be explained by the person's religious, cultural and environmental background)

   b Hallucinations that are not mood congruent – these may occur in any sensory modality

   c Catatonic symptoms, for example stupor, posturing, waxy flexibility, negativism

   d 'Negative' symptoms, where there is definite evidence that these are a change from the individual's premorbid state/baseline functioning, for example apathy, loss of adaptive skills, impairment of goal-directed behaviour, flattening or incongruity of emotional responses

   e Disordered form of thought, where there is definite evidence that this is a change from the individual's premorbid state.

Note 1: The term schizophrenic/delusional disorder, currently in episode [IIIB3.1i]; [–]; [–] should be used (in place of schizophrenic/delusional episode) if the person has additionally experienced a previous DC–LD schizophrenic/delusional episode, or alternatively if they have continuously met DC–LD criteria for schizophrenic/delusional episode for at least the past six months.

Note 2: The term schizophrenic/delusional disorder, partial remission [IIIB3.1ii]; [equivalent to F20. x4]; [–] should be used (in place of schizophrenic/delusional episode) when the person has had two previous DC–LD schizophrenic/delusional episodes and now has some remaining symptoms insufficient to meet DC–LD criteria. This term should also be used when the person has had one previous episode that continuously met DC–LD schizophrenic/delusional episode criteria for at least a six-month period and now has some remaining symptoms insufficient to meet DC–LD criteria.

Note 3: The term schizophrenic/delusional disorder, complete remission [IIIB3.1iii]; [equivalent to F20. x5]; [–] should be used (in place of schizophrenic/delusional episode) when the person is currently in complete remission, but has had two previous DC–LD schizophrenic/delusional episodes, or one previous episode that continuously met DC–LD schizophrenic/delusional episode criteria for at least a six-month period.

IIIB3.2xx Schizoaffective episode

A   The symptoms/signs must not be a direct consequence of other psychiatric disorders (e.g. dementia or delirium), prescribed or illegal drugs or alcohol or physical disorders such as thyroid dysfunction.

B   Both items 1 and 2 must be present within the same episode, and concurrently for at least part of the episode:
   1   The symptoms/signs within this episode meet criteria A, D, E, and F for depressive episode, manic episode or mixed affective episode (pages 44–48).
   2   The symptoms/signs within this episode meet criterion C for schizophrenic/delusional episode (page 39).

C Symptoms from both B1 and B2 must be prominent in the clinical picture (diagnosis depends upon an approximate 'balance' between the number, severity and duration of the schizophrenic/delusional and affective symptoms).

Note 1: The term schizoaffective disorder, currently in episode [IIIB3.2i]; [–]; |–| should be used (in place of schizoaffective episode) if the person has additionally experienced a previous DC–LD schizoaffective episode, or alternatively if they have continuously met DC–LD criteria for schizoaffective episode for at least the past six months.

Note 2: The term schizoaffective disorder, in remission [IIIB3.2ii]; [–]; |–| should be used (in place of schizo-affective episode) when the person is currently in remission, but has had two previous DC–LD schizo-affective episodes or one previous episode that continuously met DC–LD criteria for schizoaffective episode for at least a six-month period.

Note 3: The suffix depressive type [IIIB3.2*x*a]; [equivalent to F25.1]; |–|, manic type [IIIB3.2*x*b]; [equivalent to F25.0]; |–| or mixed type [IIIB3.2*x*c]; [equivalent to F25.2]; |–| should be used to specify the type of episode (i.e. the relevant criteria applied in item B1 of schizo-affective episode), for example, schizoaffective episode, depressive type [IIIB3.2a]; schizoaffective disorder, currently in episode, manic type [IIIB3.2ib].

IIIB3.3   Other non-affective psychotic disorders

This is a residual category for non-affective psychotic disorders that do not meet the criteria for any of the categories above, or other categories in ICD–10, for example, peri-ictal psychosis.

Other ICD–10 non-affective psychotic disorders

The following ICD–10 psychotic disorders may be relevant in certain conditions, for example, psychotic symptoms secondary to hyperthyroidism. Please note that these categories should *not* be used purely because the person with non-affective psychosis has learning disabilities, has epilepsy, or because there is an underlying cause for his or her learning disabilities that is associated with a behavioural phenotype that includes psychosis (as described more fully in the section headed 'ICD–10 'organic' disorders'). The ICD–10 manuals should be consulted for details of diagnostic criteria if use of these categories is considered (one of the requirements of these criteria is that there is recovery from or significant improvement in the mental disorder following removal or improvement of the underlying presumed cause):

- Organic hallucinosis [F06.0]; [equivalent to 293.82]
- Organic catatonic disorder [F06.1]; [equivalent to 293.89]
- Organic delusional (schizophrenic-like) disorder [F06.2]; [equivalent to 293.82]

Other types of psychotic disorders are included in ICD–10. In general, the application of such criteria requires a higher level of verbal communication skills than are likely to be present in the group of people at whom the use of DC–LD is aimed. However, in some circumstances these categories may be useful; the ICD–10 manuals should be consulted for more details of diagnostic criteria if use of these categories is considered:

- Paranoid schizophrenia [F20.0x]; [equivalent to 295.30]
- Hebephrenic schizophrenia [F20.1x]; [equivalent to 295.10]
- Catatonic schizophrenia [F20.2x]; [equivalent to 295.20]
- Undifferentiated schizophrenia [F20.3x]; [equivalent to 295.90]
- Residual schizophrenia [F20.5x]; [equivalent to 295.60]
- Schizotypal disorder [F21]; [equivalent to 301.22]
- Delusional disorder [F22.0]; [equivalent to 297.1]
- Other persistent delusional disorders [F22.8]; [–]
- Acute polymorphic psychotic disorder without symptoms of schizophrenia [F23.0x]; [equivalent to 298.8]
- Acute polymorphic psychotic disorder with symptoms of schizophrenia [F23.1x]; [equivalent to 298.8]
- Acute schizophrenia-like psychotic disorder [F23.2x]; [equivalent to 298.8]
- Other acute predominately delusional psychotic disorders [F23.3x]; [equivalent to 298.8]
- Other acute and transient psychotic disorders [F23.8x]; [equivalent to 298.8]
- Acute and transient psychotic disorder, unspecified [F23.9x]; [equivalent to 298.8]
- Induced delusional disorder [F24]; [equivalent to 297.3]

Affective disorders: Introduction

DC–LD includes the following disorders in this group:

- IIIB4.1*xx* Depressive episode; bipolar affective disorder; recurrent depressive disorder [equivalent to F32.*xx*, F31.3, F31.4, F31.5, F33.*xx*]; [equivalent to 296.2*x*, 296.5*x*, 296.89 (depressed), 296.3*x*]
- IIIB4.2*xx* Manic episode; bipolar affective disorder [equivalent to F30.*x*, F31.0, F31.1, F31.2]; [equivalent to 296.0*x*, 296.40, 296.4*x*, 296.89 (hypomanic)]
- IIIB4.3*xx* Mixed affective episode; bipolar affective disorder [equivalent to F38.00, F31.6]; [equivalent to 296.0*x* (mixed), 296.6*x*]
- IIIB4.4 Other specified mood (affective) disorders [F38.8]; [equivalent to 296.90]
- Other ICD–10 affective disorders

These disorders may occur at different times in the same person. Some people may experience a single depressive episode in their lifetime. Others may experience recurrent depressive episodes, in which case they can be said to have a recurrent depressive disorder. Some people may experience two (or more) out of depressive, manic or mixed affective episodes at different times – the term bipolar affective disorder, followed by a specification of the current episode may be used in these cases. In this way, DC–LD follows the same approach to classification of affective disorders as the ICD–10 manuals.

The nosological status of mixed affective episode is uncertain. These are episodes that simultaneously include symptoms commonly found in depressive episodes and symptoms commonly found in manic episodes, with neither symptom type predominating. Some psychiatrists consider such presentations to be a variant of depressive episodes, and employ treatment approaches similar to those for the treatment of depression. Conversely, the ICD–10 manuals classify such disorders, when recurrent, within the bipolar affective disorder group. Further research is required to better understand the nature of such disorders. Mixed affective episodes appear to occur more commonly among adults with learning disabilities than they do among the general population.

For the diagnosis of affective disorders, information is required from a reliable informant who has known the person with learning disabilities for a long period of time, as psychopathology can only be regarded as symptomatic if it represents a change from a person's usual premorbid state, that is, distinguishing state (symptoms of mood episodes) from traits (long-standing behaviours or personality characteristics). A pertinent example of this would be the case of a person with autism who develops a superimposed depressive episode: it would be important to distinguish whether the person's social withdrawal was a long-standing trait of his or her autism, or a new symptom as part of a depressive episode. Onset of, or increase in, problem behaviours are common in depressive episodes, for example aggression or self-injurious behaviour.

Drugs or other physical disorders must be excluded as the cause of the presentation, for example hypothyroidism. Physical disorders can coexist with affective disorders – indeed there is probably an association, with affective disorders being more common among those with physical disorders than in those without. However, where there is a presumed aetiological relationship, it must be considered whether it is more appropriate to view psychopathology as part of a physical disorder or as a separate additional psychiatric disorder. This requires clinical training, skill and experience.

When undertaking a psychiatric assessment, diagnosis must be based on the presenting psychopathology, with the presumed aetiological factors being derived from the rest of the assessment. Some information may increase the likelihood of a person's diagnosis being that of an affective disorder. Examples include the person having had a past history of mania or depression, or of there being a strong family history of affective disorder. However, while such information may be useful to a health professional when designing a person's treatment care plan, particularly when assessment of psychopathology has left some diagnostic doubt, this information cannot itself form part of the diagnostic criteria. This is because it does not relate to the person's present state – it is clinical information that is always part of that person, both when they currently have a present state diagnosis and also when they are free from a present state diagnosis (i.e. between episodes).

IIIB4.1xx   Depressive episode

A   The symptoms/signs must be present **nearly every day for at least two weeks**.

B   They must not be a direct consequence of drugs or other physical disorders, for example, hypothyroidism.

C The criteria for mixed affective episode or schizoaffective episode are not met. (Hierarchically, mixed affective episode and schizoaffective episode take precedence over depressive episode.)

D The symptoms/signs must each represent a change from the individual's premorbid state.

E Item 1 *or* 2 must be present and prominent:
   1 Depressed mood (i.e. misery; failure to maintain the persons usual mood state throughout the day)
      Or Irritable mood (e.g. onset of or increase in physical/verbal aggression in response to minor things that the person would usually take in his or her stride; reduced level of tolerance)
   2 Loss of interest or pleasure in activities (failure to enjoy activities that were previously enjoyed, or less time engaged in activities/interests previously enjoyed)
      Or Social withdrawal (reduced social interaction; reduction in initiation of social interaction or increased withdrawal from social approaches made by others)
      Or Reduction of self-care (reduced inclination to use self-care skills; or apparent loss of self-care skills; or refusal to cooperate with the usual physical care provided by others)
      Or Reduction in the quantity of speech/communication.

F Some of the following symptoms must be present, so that at least four symptoms from E and F are present in total:
   1 Loss of energy; increased lethargy
   2 Loss of confidence
      Or Increase in reassurance-seeking behaviour/onset of or increase in anxiety or fearfulness
   3 Increased tearfulness
   4 Onset of or increase in somatic symptoms/physical health concerns (e.g. increased complaints of many aches or pains; increased preoccupation with physical illness; repeatedly showing different parts of the body for carer to check)
   5 Reduced ability to concentrate/distractibility
      Or Increased indecisiveness
   6 Increase in a specific problem behaviour
   7 Increased motor agitation
      Or Increased motor retardation

Axis III
DC–LD Level B

45

8   Onset of or increase in appetite disturbance (i.e. loss of appetite or increase in appetite)
    Or Significant weight change (i.e. loss of weight or weight gain of at least seven pounds/5% of body weight)

9   Onset of or increase in sleep disturbance (i.e. a delay in getting off to sleep of at least one hour more than usual; broken sleep, with the person waking in the night for at least an hour more than usual; and/or waking at least an hour earlier in the morning than usual).

Note 1: The term bipolar affective disorder, current episode depression [IIIB4.1i]; [equivalent to F31.3*x*, F31.4, F31.5*x*]; [equivalent to 296.5*x* (where *x* is 1–4), 296.89 (currently depressed)] should be used (in place of depressive episode) if the person has additionally experienced a previous DC–LD manic or mixed affective episode.

Note 2: The term bipolar affective disorder, currently in remission [IIIB4.1ii]; [equivalent to F31.7]; [equivalent to 296.56, 296.46, 296.66, 296.76, 296.89 (in remission)] should be used (in place of depressive episode) if the person is currently in remission but has experienced at least two previous DC–LD affective episodes, at least one of which was a manic or mixed affective episode.

Note 3: The term recurrent depressive disorder, currently in episode [IIIB4.1iii]; [equivalent to F33.0*x*, F33.1*x*, F33.2, F33.3*x*]; [equivalent to 296.3*x* (where *x* is 1–3] should be used (in place of depressive episode) if the person has additionally experienced a previous DC–LD depressive episode.

Note 4: The term recurrent depressive disorder, currently in remission [IIIB4.1iv]; [equivalent to F33.4]; [equivalent to 296.36] should be used (in place of depressive episode) if the person is in remission but has experienced at least two previous DC–LD depressive episodes.

Note 5: The suffix with psychotic symptoms [IIIB4.1*x*a]; [F32.3*x*, F31.5*x*, F33.3*x*]; [equivalent to 296.54, 296.34] or without psychotic symptoms [IIIB4.1*x*b]; [equivalent to F32.2, F31.4, F33.2]; [equivalent to 296.53, 296.33] should be used to specify symptom subtypes, for example, bipolar affective disorder, current episode depression without psychotic symptoms [IIIB4.1ib].

IIIB4.2xx Manic episode

A The symptom/signs must be present for **at least one week**.

B They must not be a direct consequence of drugs or other physical disorders, for example, hyperthyroidism.

C The criteria for mixed affective episode or schizoaffective episode are not met. (Hierarchically, mixed affective episode and schizoaffective episode take precedence over manic episode.)

D The symptom/signs must represent a change from the person's premorbid state.

E An abnormally elevated, expansive or irritable mood must be present (e.g. irritability may be demonstrated by onset of or increase in physical/verbal aggression in response to minor things that the person would usually take in his or her stride; reduced level of tolerance).

F Three of the following symptoms must additionally be present:
1 Onset of or increase in overactivity; excessive energy
2 Increased talkativeness (or increased vocalisation)/ pressure of speech
3 Flight of ideas
4 Loss of usual social inhibitions (excluding sexual inhibitions) and inappropriate social behaviour (e.g. talking to strangers; over-familiarity; intrusive-ness, such as talking across others' conversation; engaging in non-sexual bodily functions in public, such as urinating, when such behaviours are out of keeping with the persons usual discretion)
5 Reduced sleep (i.e. sleeping for at least an hour less than usual)
6 Increase in self-esteem such that it is over-inflated; or grandiosity
7 Reduced concentration/distractibility
8 Reckless behaviour (e.g. impaired judgement compared with that usual for the person such that he or she engages in activities usually avoided. This might include excessive spending of money, giving away belongings, placing themselves in danger)
9 Increased libido/sexual energy, or sexual indiscretions that are out of keeping with the person's usual behaviour (e.g. masturbating in public; touching others in a sexual way).

Note 1: The term bipolar affective disorder, current episode manic [IIIB4.2i]; [equivalent to F31.0, F31.1, F31.2*x*]; [equivalent to 296.40 (currently manic), 296.4*x* (where *x* is 1–4), 296.89 (currently hypomanic)] should be used (in place of manic episode) if the person has additionally experienced a previous DC–LD depressive, manic or mixed affective episode.

Note 2: The term bipolar affective disorder, currently in remission [IIIB4.1ii]; [equivalent to F31.7]; [equivalent to 296.56, 296.46, 296.66, 296.76, 296.89 (in remission)] should be used (in place of manic episode) if the person is currently in remission but has experienced at least two previous DC–LD affective episodes, at least one of which was a manic or mixed affective episode.

Note 3: The suffix with psychotic symptoms [IIIB4.2*x*a]; [equivalent to F30.2*x*, F31.2*x*]; [equivalent to 296.04, 296.44] or without psychotic symptoms [IIIB4.2*x*b]; [equivalent to F30.1, F31.1]; [equivalent to 296.03, 296.43] should be used to specify symptom subtypes, for example, bipolar affective disorder, current episode manic without psychotic symptoms [IIIB4.2ib].

IIIB4.3*xx* Mixed affective episode

A   The symptoms/signs must be present **nearly every day for at least two weeks**.

B   They must not be a direct consequence of drugs or other physical disorders, for example, hypothyroidism.

C   The criteria for schizoaffective episode are not met. (Hierarchically, schizoaffective episode takes precedence over mixed affective disorder.)

D   The symptoms/signs must represent a change from the individual's premorbid state.

E   Labile mood must be present (i.e. onset of or increase in mood lability, demonstrated as rapid alteration between misery/depression and elevated, expansive or irritable mood. Rapid alteration refers to changes every few minutes or hours).

F   The symptoms/signs within this episode must meet the criteria for *both* depressive episode (pages 44–46) and manic episode (pages 47).

Note 1: The term bipolar affective disorder, current episode mixed [IIIB4.3i]; [equivalent to F31.6]; [equivalent to 296.6x (where x is 1–4)] should be used (in place of mixed affective episode) if the person has additionally experienced a previous DC–LD depressive, manic or mixed affective episode.

Note 2: The term bipolar affective disorder, currently in remission [IIIB4.1ii]; [equivalent to F31.7]; [equivalent to 296.56, 296.46, 296.66, 296.76, 296.89 (in remission)] should be used (in place of mixed affective episode) if the person is currently in remission but has experienced at least two previous DC–LD affective episodes, at least one of which was a manic or mixed affective episode.

Note 3: The suffix with psychotic symptoms [IIIB4.3xa]; [–]; [equivalent to 296.64] or without psychotic symptoms [IIIB4.3xb]; [–]; [equivalent to 296.63] should be used to specify symptom subtypes, for example, bipolar affective disorder, current episode mixed without psychotic symptoms [IIIB4.3ib].

IIIB4.4   Other specified mood (affective) disorders

This is a residual category for affective disorders that do not meet the criteria for any of the categories above, or other categories in ICD–10.

Other ICD–10 affective disorders

The following ICD–10 affective disorders may be relevant in certain conditions, for example affective symptoms secondary to hyperthyroidism. Please note that these categories should *not* be used purely because the person with affective symptoms has learning disabilities, has epilepsy, or because there is an underlying cause for his or her learning disabilities that is associated with a behavioural phenotype that includes affective symptoms (as described more fully in the section headed 'ICD–10 'organic' disorders'). The ICD–10 manuals should be consulted for details of diagnostic criteria if use of these categories is considered (one of the requirements of these criteria is that there is recovery from or significant improvement in the mental disorder following removal or improvement of the underlying presumed cause):

- Organic manic disorder [F06.30]; [equivalent to 293.83]
- Organic bipolar disorder [F06.31]; [equivalent to 293.83]
- Organic depressive disorder [F06.32]; [equivalent to 293.83]
- Organic mixed affective disorder [F06.35]; [equivalent to 293.83]

Other types of affective disorders are included in ICD–10. The ICD–10 manuals should be consulted for details of diagnostic criteria if use of these categories is considered:

- Other depressive episodes [F32.8]; [–]
- Cyclothymia [F34.0]; [equivalent to 301.13]
- Dysthymia [F34.1]; [equivalent to 300.4]
- Other persistent mood (affective) disorders [F34.8]; [–]
- Persistent mood (affective) disorder, unspecified [F34.9]; [–]
- Other recurrent mood (affective) disorders [F38.10]; [–] Includes recurrent brief depressive disorder.

Neurotic and stress-related disorders: Introduction

DC–LD includes the following disorders in this group:

- IIIB5.1x   Agoraphobia [equivalent to F40.00, F40.01]; [equivalent to 300.21, 300.22]
- IIIB5.2   Social phobia [equivalent to F40.1]; [equivalent to 300.23]
- IIIB5.3   Specific phobias [equivalent to F40.2]; [equivalent to 300.29]
- IIIB5.4   Panic disorder [equivalent to F41.0]; [equivalent to 300.01]
- IIIB5.5   Generalised anxiety disorder [equivalent to F41.1]; [equivalent to 300.02]
- IIIB5.6   Other specified anxiety disorders [F41.8]; [equivalent to 300.00]
- IIIB5.7   Other phobic anxiety disorders[F40.8]; [equivalent to 300.00]
- IIIB5.8   Obsessive–compulsive disorder [equivalent to F42.x];[equivalent to 300.3]
- IIIB5.9   Acute stress reaction [equivalent to F43.0x]; [equivalent to 308.3]
- IIIB5.10   Adjustment disorders [equivalent to F43.2x]; [equivalent to 309.0, 309.2x, 309.3, 309.4, 309.9]

- IIIB5.11   Other reactions to severe stress [F43.8]; [−]
- Other ICD–10 neurotic and stress-related disorders

Anxiety disorders are probably common among adults with learning disabilities, although it is likely that many are undiagnosed and untreated. Often, there is a long history, sometimes extending back into childhood, and it may be impossible to date the time at which symptoms of anxiety first appeared. To satisfy diagnostic criteria, either the symptoms of anxiety or the avoidance caused by anticipatory anxiety (in the case of phobic anxiety disorders) must be sufficiently severe or frequent to cause suffering to the individual. Occasional anxiety symptoms in situations in which most people would find themselves anxious would not be sufficient to warrant a diagnosis of an anxiety disorder. Many features of anxiety are readily observable in people with learning disabilities and are similar to those seen in the general population (for example, appearing frightened, sweating, trembling or becoming flushed), but ICD–10 criteria tend to rely on the subjective description of such symptoms. In DC–LD, *either* the person's subjective description of the symptom *or* its observation by others are included in the criteria. This allows the diagnosis of anxiety disorders in those people with learning disabilities who are unable to describe such symptoms, because of either limited intellect or limited verbal skills.

Persons with learning disabilities are usually unable to describe the more complex cognitive phenomena that occur in anxiety disorders, for example, depersonalisation and derealisation. Such features have therefore been excluded. In the case of the phobias, DC–LD criteria do not require individuals to recognise their fear to be excessive and unreasonable as most people with learning disabilities are unable to describe their symptoms with this degree of insight. However, there is a specific exclusion that the anxiety is not secondary to other psychiatric disorders, particularly psychosis. Avoidance of specific situations may not be prominent in people with learning disabilities, as they may have limited opportunities to make or display such choices.

While cognitive features of the anxiety disorders are infrequently elicited in people with learning disabilities, behavioural features are often seen. Irritability and restless-ness are commonly observed in people with learning disabilities as symptoms of anxiety, and can be marked. These symptoms have been included in the criteria for all the anxiety disorders. Irritability may present as aggression towards self or others or destructiveness to property, and can be a prominent part of the clinical presentation of anxiety disorders, particularly in those people who are unable to describe their worries and fears.

Before making a diagnosis of one of the anxiety disorders, it is essential to exclude physical illnesses or other psychiatric disorders as the main cause of the anxiety symptoms. Other psychiatric disorders that may cause symptoms of anxiety include schizophrenia and other psychotic disorders, depression and obsessive–compulsive disorder. However, comorbidity can and does occur and DC–LD allows for more than one Axis III Level B diagnosis should this best describe the clinical picture. Social withdrawal due to pervasive developmental disorders may mimic agoraphobia or social phobia, and so must clearly be differentiated.

Many of the general points applicable to anxiety disorders are equally pertinent to the diagnosis of obsessive–compulsive disorder in people with learning disabilities. In particular, diagnostic criteria of obsessive–compulsive disorder in the general population include the description of complex cognitive phenomena that are difficult to elicit in people with learning disabilities owing to limitations in intellect and/or limited verbal skills. For instance, it is rarely possible to obtain a clear description of obsessions/compulsions being the product of a person's own mind. Consequently, DC–LD requires that there is no evidence that the person believes the obsessions/compulsions to be imposed on him or her from an external source. As in the anxiety disorders, a person with learning disabilities may not recognise or be able to describe the unreasonableness of the obsessions/compulsions, although they must be considered as being repetitive and excessive by others, if not by the person him- or herself. It is recognised that resistance to the obsessions/compulsions may be minimal or not described at all in a person with learning disabilities, particularly if they have been long-standing.

Obsessions/compulsions can arise in a number of disorders other than obsessive–compulsive disorder. If they are solely accounted for by another psychiatric illness, pervasive developmental disorder or physical disorder, they should be coded as such, and a diagnosis of obsessive–compulsive disorder should *not* be made. Compulsions must also be distinguished from the repetitive movements, most often rhythmic movements, seen frequently in some people with severe/profound learning disabilities (stereotypies). It should be noted, however, that compulsions can be associated with aggression, particularly as a result of the increase in tension or anxiety that occurs if attempts are made by others or the person him- or herself to prevent compulsions being performed.

IIIB5.1x   Agoraphobia

A   The symptoms/signs must not be a direct consequence of other psychiatric disorders (e.g. non-affective psychotic disorders, depressive episode, obsessive–compulsive disorder), drugs or physical disorders such as hyperthyroidism.

B   Marked anxiety/fear occurs in at least two of the following, or, alternatively, these situations are avoided owing to anticipatory fear, or the person runs away to escape the situation. The person may describe these experiences or alternatively his or her expression or behaviour may demonstrate anxiety or fear.
   1   Crowds
   2   Public places, for example shops, queues, cinema
   3   Using public transport
   4   Leaving the home.

C   In the feared situation, or while anticipating the feared situation, at least two items from the following occur:
   1   Palpitations or pounding or racing heartbeat
   2   Sweating
   3   Trembling or shaking
   4   Dry mouth (e.g. repeatedly asking for drinks)
   5   Difficulty breathing; hyperventilation
   6   Chest pain or discomfort
   7   Nausea, vomiting or churning stomach ('butterflies'; 'stomach turning over')
   8   Dizziness; unsteadiness
   9   Hot flushes or cold chills
   10 Restlessness
   11 Irritability due to anxiety/fear (e.g. physical/verbal aggression in the phobic situation).

> Note: The term agoraphobia with panic disorder
> [IIIB5.1a]; [equivalent to F40.00]; [equivalent to 300.21]
> or agoraphobia without panic disorder [IIIB5.1b];
> [equivalent to F40.01]; [equivalent to 300.22] may be
> used (in place of agoraphobia) to provide further clinical
> detail as to whether the person usually experiences panic
> attacks in agoraphobic situations.

IIIB5.2 Social phobia

A   Symptoms/signs must not be a direct consequence of other psychiatric disorders (e.g. depressive episode, agoraphobia or obsessive–compulsive disorder), drugs or physical disorders such as hyperthyroidism.

B   Anxiety/fear occurs in social situations, for example eating in public, attending parties, meetings, work, when the person is the focus of attention; or, alternatively, these situations are avoided owing to anticipatory fears, or the person runs away to escape the situation. The person may describe fear of behaving in a way that will be embarrassing or humiliating, or alternatively his or her expression or behaviour may demonstrate anxiety or fear in these situations.

C   In the feared situation, or in anticipation of the feared situation, one of the following items must occur:
1   Blushing or shaking
2   Vomiting, retching or fear of vomiting
3   Urgency of micturition or defecation, or incontinence.

D   Additionally, in the feared situation, or in anticipation of the feared situation, at least two items from the following occur:
1   Palpitations or pounding or racing heartbeat
2   Sweating
3   Trembling or shaking
4   Dry mouth (e.g. repeatedly asking for drinks)
5   Difficulty breathing; hyperventilation
6   Chest pain or discomfort
7   Nausea, vomiting or churning stomach ('butterflies'; 'stomach turning over')
8   Dizziness; unsteadiness
9   Hot flushes or cold chills

10 Restlessness

11 Irritability due to anxiety/fear (e.g. physical/verbal aggression in the phobic situation).

IIIB5.3   Specific phobias

A   The symptoms/signs are not secondary to non-affective psychotic disorder.

B   Anxiety/fear occurs in association with a specific situation or object, or, alternatively, these situations/objects are avoided owing to anticipatory fear, or the person runs away to escape the situation (e.g. cats, dogs, insects, thunder, heights, injections).

C   In the feared situation or in contact with the feared object, or in anticipation of the situation/object, at least two items from the following occur:
1   Palpitations or pounding or racing heartbeat
2   Sweating
3   Trembling or shaking
4   Dry mouth (e.g. repeatedly asking for drinks)
5   Difficulty breathing; hyperventilation
6   Chest pain or discomfort
7   Nausea, vomiting or churning stomach ('butterflies'; 'stomach turning over')
8   Dizziness; unsteadiness
9   Hot flushes or cold chills
10   Restlessness
11   Irritability due to anxiety/fear (e.g. physical/verbal aggression in the phobic situation).

IIIB5.4   Panic disorder

A   The person experiences recurrent panic attacks. **At least four panic attacks** should have occurred **within a one-month period** in unpredictable circumstances.

B   The panic attacks are not a direct consequence of other psychiatric disorders (e.g. non-affective psychotic disorders, depressive episode or phobic disorders), drugs or physical disorders such as hyperthyroidism, or epilepsy.

C   The panic attacks must have the following characteristics:
1   A discrete episode of intense fear. The person may describe this experience or alternatively his or her

expression or behaviour may demonstrate anxiety or fear

2 Abrupt onset

3 Maximal within a few minutes.

D Three of the following items must be present during the panic attack:

1 Palpitations or pounding or racing heartbeat

2 Sweating

3 Trembling or shaking

4 Dry mouth (e.g. repeatedly asking for drinks)

5 Difficulty breathing; hyperventilation

6 Chest pain or discomfort

7 Nausea, vomiting or churning stomach ('butterflies'; 'stomach turning over')

8 Dizziness; unsteadiness

9 Hot flushes or cold chills

10 Restlessness

11 Irritability due to anxiety/fear (e.g. physical/verbal aggression in response to things that the person would usually take in his or her stride; reduced level of tolerance).

IIIB5.5   Generalised anxiety disorder

A The symptoms/signs must be present **on most days for at least six months**, although they may be long-standing.

B The symptoms/signs must not be a direct consequence of other psychiatric disorder (e.g. non-affective psychotic disorders, depressive episode, phobic anxiety disorders, panic disorder or obsessive–compulsive disorder), drugs or physical disorders such as hyperthyroidism, epilepsy or cardiac disorder.

C The anxiety is generalised, and not restricted to any particular environmental circumstance (i.e. it is free-floating).

D The person experiences prominent tension, worry or feelings of apprehension about everyday events and problems. The person may describe these experiences, or alternatively his or her expression or behaviour may demonstrate anxiety or fear.

E Additionally, at least one of items 1–4 must be present:
1 Palpitations or pounding or racing heartbeat
2 Sweating
3 Trembling or shaking
4 Dry mouth (e.g. repeatedly asking for drinks).

F Some of the following symptoms may also be present so
that at least three symptoms from E and F are present in
total:
1 Difficulty breathing; hyperventilation
2 Chest pain or discomfort
3 Nausea, vomiting or churning stomach ('butterflies';
'stomach turning over')
4 Dizziness; unsteadiness
5 Hot flushes or cold chills
6 Tense muscles (e.g. aching shoulders/back; tension
headache)
7 Restlessness
8 Lump in throat; repeated swallowing
9 Exaggerated response to minor surprises or being
startled
10 Difficulty concentrating; distractibility
11 Irritability due to anxiety/fear (e.g. physical/verbal
aggression in response to things that the person
would usually take in his or her stride; reduced level of
tolerance)
12 Initial insomnia, due to worry, anxiety or fear.

IIIB5.6 Other specified anxiety disorders

This is a residual category for anxiety disorders that do not
meet the criteria for any of the categories above, or other
categories in ICD–10.

IIIB5.7 Other phobic anxiety disorders

This is a residual category for phobic anxiety disorders that do
not meet the criteria for any of the categories above, or other
categories in ICD–10.

IIIB5.8 Obsessive–compulsive disorder

A Obsessions and/or compulsions are present **on most days
for at least two weeks**. They may be long-standing.

B   They are not a direct consequence of another psychiatric disorder (e.g. pervasive developmental disorders, non-affective psychotic disorders, depressive episode), drugs or physical disorder.

C   The obsessions (thoughts, ideas or images) and compulsions (acts e.g. cleaning, washing, checking, orderliness, tidiness) have the following features:
1   There is no evidence the person believes the obsessions or compulsions to be imposed by outside persons or influences
2   They are repetitive and excessive
3   They are unpleasant or purposeless and not inherently enjoyable (temporary relief of tension/ anxiety should not be viewed as enjoyment)
4   The person may try to resist them – but there may be no resistant to long-standing obsessions or compulsions
5   Interference with the person's compulsions causes him or her distress, which may be associated with aggression.

D   The obsessions or compulsions cause distress, or interfere with the person's social or individual functioning, usually by wasting time.

IIIB5.9   Acute stress reaction

A   Exposure to an exceptional mental or physical stressor (e.g. assault, rape, natural catastrophe) is followed by an immediate onset of symptoms (within an hour).

B   Symptoms **begin to diminish within 72 hours** (whether or not the stressor was transient or is continuous).

C   The symptoms/signs must not be a direct consequence of other psychiatric disorder (e.g. non-affective psychotic disorders, depressive episode, phobic anxiety disorders, panic disorder, generalised anxiety disorder, obsessive–compulsive disorder), drugs or physical disorders such as hypothyroidism.

D   The symptoms/signs must represent a change from the individual's premorbid state.

E   At least one of the following symptoms occur:
1   Palpitations or pounding or racing heartbeat
2   Sweating

3 Trembling or shaking

4 Dry mouth (e.g. repeatedly asking for drinks).

F Some of the following symptoms may also be present, so that at least three symptoms from E and F are present in total:

1 Difficulty breathing; hyperventilation

2 Chest pain or discomfort

3 Nausea, vomiting or churning stomach ('butterflies'; 'stomach turning over')

4 Dizziness; unsteadiness

5 Hot flushes or cold chills

6 Tense muscles (e.g. aching shoulders/back; tension headache)

7 Restlessness

8 Lump in throat; repeated swallowing

9 Exaggerated response to minor surprises or being startled

10 Difficulty concentrating; distractibility

11 Irritability due to anxiety/fear (e.g. physical/verbal aggression in response to things that the person would usually take in his or her stride; reduced level of tolerance)

12 Initial insomnia, due to worry, anxiety or fear.

> Note: When severe, acute stress reaction may include social withdrawal, reduced level of attention, reduced orientation, over-activity or excessive grief.

IIIB5.10   Adjustment disorders

A Exposure to an identified psychosocial stressor is followed within a month by onset of symptoms.

B Symptoms must not continue for more than six months after cessation of the stress.

C The symptoms/signs must not be a direct consequence of other psychiatric disorders (e.g. non-affective psychotic disorder, depressive episode, generalised anxiety disorder), drugs or physical disorders such as hypothyroidism.

D The symptoms/signs must represent a change from the individual's premorbid state.

E   Symptoms occur such as those found in depressive episode, manic episode, mixed affective episode (except delusions and hallucinations), agoraphobia, panic disorder, generalised anxiety disorder and obsessive–compulsive disorder, but the criteria for an individual disorder are not fulfilled. Symptoms may be variable in both form and severity.

IIIB5.11   Other reactions to severe stress

This is a residual category for stress-related disorders that do not meet the criteria for any of the categories above, or other categories in ICD–10.

Other ICD–10 neurotic and stress-related disorders

The following neurotic and stress-related disorders may be relevant in certain conditions, for example, anxiety symptoms secondary to hyperthyroidism. Please note that these categories should *not* be used purely because the person with a neurotic or stress-related disorder has learning disabilities, has epilepsy, or because there is an underlying cause for his or her learning disabilities that is associated with a behavioural phenotype that includes neurotic and stress-related disorders (as described more fully in the section headed 'ICD–10 'organic' disorders'). The ICD–10 manuals should be consulted for details of diagnostic criteria if use of these categories is considered (one of the requirements of these criteria is that there is recovery from or significant improvement in the mental disorder following removal or improvement of the underlying presumed cause):

- Organic anxiety disorder [F06.4]; [equivalent to 293.89]
- Organic emotionally labile (asthenic) disorder [F06.6]; [equivalent to 293.89]

Other types of neurotic and stress-related disorders are included in ICD–10. The ICD–10 manuals should be consulted for details of diagnostic criteria if use of these categories is considered:

- Mixed anxiety and depressive disorder [F41.2]; [equivalent to 300.00]
- Other mixed anxiety disorder [F41.3]; [equivalent to 300.00]
- Post traumatic stress disorder [F43.1]; [equivalent to 309.81]

- Dissociative amnesia [F44.0]; [equivalent to 300.12]
- Dissociative fugue [F44.1]; [equivalent to 300.13]
- Dissociative stupor [F44.2]; [equivalent to 300.15]
- Trance and possession disorders [F44.3]; [equivalent to 300.15]
- Dissociative motor disorders [F44.4]; [equivalent to 300.11]
- Dissociative convulsions [F44.5]; [equivalent to 300.11]
- Dissociative anaesthesia and sensory loss [F44.6]; [equivalent to 300.11]
- Mixed dissociative (conversion) disorder [F44.7]; [equivalent to 300.11]
- Other dissociative (conversion) disorder [F44.8x]; [300.14, equivalent to 300.15]
  Includes Ganser's syndrome; multiple personality disorder.
- Somatisation disorder [F45.0]; [equivalent to 300.81]
- Undifferentiated somatoform disorder [F45.1]; [equivalent to 300.81]
- Hypochondriacal disorder [F45.2]; [equivalent to 300.7]
- Somatoform autonomic disorder [F45.3]; [equivalent to 300.81]
- Persistent somatoform pain disorder [F45.4]; [equivalent to 307.80, 307.89]
- Other somatoform disorders [F45.8]; [equivalent to 300.81]
- Neurasthenia [F48.0]; [–]
- Depersonalisation–derealisation syndrome [F48.1]; [equivalent to 300.6, 300.15]
- Other specified neurotic disorders [F48.8]; [–].

Eating disorders: Introduction

DC–LD includes the following disorders in this group:

- IIIB6.1   Anorexia nervosa [equivalent to F50.0, F50.1]; [equivalent to 307.1; 307.50]
- IIIB6.2   Bulimia nervosa [equivalent to F50.2, F50.3]; [equivalent to 307.51; 307.50]
- IIIB6.3   Binge eating disorder [equivalent to F50.8]; [equivalent to 307.50]
- IIIB6.4x   Psychogenic over-eating episode; psychogenic over-eating disorder [equivalent to F50.4]; [–]
- IIIB6.5x   Psychogenic vomiting episode; psychogenic vomiting disorder [equivalent to F50.5]; [–]

- IIIB6.6*x*   Psychogenic loss of appetite episode; psychogenic loss of appetite disorder [equivalent to F50.8]; [–]
- IIIB6.7   Food faddiness/food refusal disorder [equivalent to F50.8, F98.2]; [equivalent to 307.59, 307.50]
- IIIB6.8   Food rumination/regurgitation disorder [equivalent to F50.8, F98.2]; [equivalent to 307.53, 307.50]
- IIIB6.9   Pica [equivalent to F50.8, F98.3, F7*x*.12]; [equivalent to 307.52]
- IIIB6.10   Excessive chewing/spitting out food disorder [equivalent to F50.8]; [equivalent to 307.50]

Despite increasing focus on the nutrition of adults with learning disabilities there has been less interest in diagnosable eating disorders. Weight and Body Mass Index (BMI) surveys (BMI = weight in kilograms/height in metres squared i.e. kg/m^2) have found that 2–35% of adults with learning disabilities are obese (BMI >30), while 5–50% are significantly underweight (BMI <17). The contribution of diagnosable eating disorders to these figures is unknown. Existing studies suggest that 5–42% of institutionalised adults with learning disabilities and 1–20% of adults with learning disabilities living in the community may have diagnosable eating disorders. The true prevalence of eating disorders is yet to be established, as is the development of multi-factorial aetiological, assessment and treatment models. The DC–LD consensus diagnostic criteria for eating disorders in adults with learning disabilities could be used to support such research, as well as being used in clinical practice.

The existing coding for the types of eating disorders found among adults with learning disabilities in the ICD–10 manuals is confused and dislocated between several parts of the manuals. The ICD–10–MR only provides diagnostic criteria for typical (F50.0) and atypical (F50.1) anorexia nervosa and bulimia nervosa (F50.2) in people with learning disabilities. Such eating disorders may be associated with Down's syndrome and Turner's syndrome and are thought to be less frequent than psychogenic over-eating, psychogenic vomiting and food faddiness/food refusal disorders in people with learning disabilities, which are not described in the ICD–10–MR. ICD–10–MR also implies that the main diagnostic guidelines for feeding disorder of infancy and childhood (F98.2: which include rumination/regurgitation, food faddiness/refusal) and pica of infancy and childhood (F98.3) could be used for these eating disorders when they occur in adults with learning disabilities. Within ICD–10–CDDG and ICD–10–DCR, these eating disorders in adults would be classified as other eating disorders (F50.8). The ICD–10 manuals also allow pica to be classified as a type of impairment of behaviour alongside the coding for severity of mental retardation (F70–F79). The ICD–10 manuals also mention psychogenic loss of appetite under other eating disorders (F50.8), but without providing diagnostic criteria. Binge eating disorder, which is considered common in dieting overweight women of average ability, is described in DSM–IV but does not feature in the ICD–10 manuals.

Many adults with learning disabilities will not possess adequate verbal communication and abstract body concept-ualisation skills to describe the complex psychopathology required to diagnose typical anorexia nervosa or bulimia nervosa when using general population criteria. This suggests that modified criteria are appropriate, as particularly atypical types of such disorders do occur in this group.

As discussed in the earlier section 'Special issues in developing DC–LD', the ICD–10 manuals do not address the issue of classification around behavioural phenotypes. They do not provide consistent guidelines on the hierarchical classification of abnormal eating behaviours that may present clinically: as part of behavioural phenotypes (such as Prader-Willi syndrome), physical disorders such as hiatus hernia, other psychiatric illness (such as depression), or, in association with some pervasive developmental disorders, personality disorders and problem behaviours. Given these many issues, DC–LD has grouped all eating disorders together under a single heading, which is then sub-classified. Given the abnormal eating, physical, weight, behavioural and other complex psychopathological features seen in eating disorders, they are classified as psychiatric illness on Axis III Level B within the hierarchical structure of the DC–LD. The hierarchical approach to diagnosis distinguishes eating dis-orders (Axis III Level B) from symptoms/traits of abnormal eating that are part of Axes II, or Axis III Level C or D disorders.

A similar approach to that taken for DC–LD and ICD–10 affective disorders is adopted for psychogenic over-eating, psychogenic vomiting and psychogenic loss of appetite. These should be coded as disorders when the person has experienced at least one previous similar episode. Such episodes are often recurrent (i.e. a disorder) owing to repeated psychosocial stressors. Clinical judgement may be required to differentiate these disorders from adjustment disorders: the episodic nature of the disorders and presence of a particular symptom (i.e. over-eating, vomiting, or loss of appetite) as opposed to other symptoms of anxiety are pointers to the diagnosis. Acute stress reactions differ from these disorders in terms of timescale/duration, as well as symptomatology, and the exceptionality of the psychosocial precipitant. Other eating disorders described in this section are defined on the basis of chronicity (their duration) and are unlikely to be episodic in nature.

IIIB6.1 Anorexia nervosa

A   The symptoms/signs are not a direct consequence of other psychiatric disorders (e.g. non-affective psychotic disorders, depressive episode, obsessive–compulsive disorder).

B   Binge eating (eating excessive food within a two-hour period) does *not* occur, or occurs less than twice-weekly over a three-month period.

C   There must be significant weight loss or a failure of weight gain so that the current significantly low weight is maintained. This should preferably be confirmed by a measured BMI of less than 17.5.

D   Two of the following symptoms must be present:
     1   Self-induced weight loss by avoidance of sugar, starchy, carbohydrate, protein-rich and other fattening foods
     2   Self-induced vomiting *and/or* purging with laxatives *and/or* frequent repeated prolonged exercise *and/or* using appetite-reducing, water or other slimming pills
     3   Distorted body image. Examples include: self-perception of being too fat *and/or* dread of becoming fat *and/or* self-imposed low ideal weight
     4   Sex hormonal dysfunction, that is, onset of amenorrhoea in women or loss of sexual interest and erections in men.

IIIB6.2 Bulimia nervosa

A   The symptoms/signs are not a direct consequence of other psychiatric disorders (e.g. non-affective psychotic disorders, depressive episode, obsessive–compulsive disorder).

B   Binge eating episodes (eating excessive food within a two-hour period) must occur **at least twice-weekly over a three-month period**.

C   Avoidance of weight gain must be present, by: self-induced vomiting *and*/*or* purging with laxatives *and*/*or* alternating periods of starvation *and*/*or* using appetite-reducing, water, thyroid or other slimming drugs.

D   One of the following symptoms must be present:
    1   Persistent repeated thoughts, cravings or compulsive rituals about food *and*/*or* eating
    2   Distorted body image. Examples include self-perception of being too fat, *and*/*or* dread of becoming fat, *and*/*or* self-imposed ideal (usually low) weight
    3   Previous history of anorexia nervosa.

IIIB6.3   Binge eating disorder

A   The symptoms/signs are not a direct consequence of other psychiatric disorders (e.g. non-affective psychotic disorders, depressive episode, obsessive–compulsive disorder, anorexia nervosa, bulimia nervosa).

B   Binge eating episodes (eating excessive food within a two-hour period) must have occurred **at least twice-weekly over a six-month period**.

C   The person does *not* use compensatory behaviours for self-induced weight loss, or to avoid weight gain, such as excessive exercise, self-induced vomiting, purging with laxatives, periods of starvation, etc.

D   Binge eating episodes must have at least three of the following characteristics:
    1   Eating faster than usual
    2   Eating until the person feels uncomfortably full
    3   Eating excessively when the person does not feel physically hungry
    4   The person feels disgusted with him- or herself, depressed or very guilty after the binge eating.

E   The person describes or is observed to have a lack of control over eating during the binge eating episodes.

F   The person is distressed about the binge eating episode. The person may describe these experiences, or alternatively this may be observed by others.

**Axis III
DC–LD Level B**

IIIB6.4*x*   Psychogenic over-eating episode

A   The symptoms/signs are not a direct consequence of other psychiatric disorders (e.g. depressive episode, bulimia nervosa, binge eating disorder), or physical disorders.

B   Exposure to an identified psychosocial stressor (e.g. bereavement, trauma, abuse, other life events and transitions) has resulted in the reaction of over-eating, **over a three-month period**.

C   Significant obesity is present. This should preferably be confirmed by a measured BMI of over 30.

Note 1: The term psychogenic over-eating disorder, currently in episode [IIIB6.4i]; [–]; [–] should be used (in place of psychogenic over-eating episode) if the person has experienced a previous DC–LD psychogenic over-eating episode.

Note 2: The term psychogenic over-eating disorder, currently in remission [IIIB6.4ii]; [–]; [–] should be used (in place of psychogenic over-eating episode) if the person is currently in remission, but has experienced at least two previous DC–LD psychogenic over-eating episodes.

IIIB6.5*x*   Psychogenic vomiting episode

A   The symptoms/signs are not a direct consequence of other psychiatric disorders (e.g. depressive episode, manic episode, anorexia nervosa, bulimia nervosa), drugs or physical disorders (e.g. hiatus hernia, uraemia).

B   Exposure to an identified psychosocial stressor (e.g. bereavement, trauma, abuse, other life events and transitions) has resulted in the reaction of repeated vomiting, **over a three-month period**.

C   Vomiting has been significant such that it has required medical consultation.

Note 1: The term psychogenic vomiting disorder, currently in episode [IIIB6.5i]; [–]; [–] should be used (in place of psychogenic vomiting episode) if the person has experienced a previous DC–LD psychogenic vomiting episode.

Note 2: The term psychogenic vomiting disorder, currently in remission [IIIB6.5ii]; [–]; [–] should be used (in place of psychogenic vomiting episode) if the person is currently in remission, but has experienced at least two previous DC–LD psychogenic vomiting episodes.

IIIB6.6x   Psychogenic loss of appetite episode

A   The symptoms/signs are not a direct consequence of other psychiatric disorders (e.g. depressive episode, generalised anxiety disorder, anorexia nervosa), drugs or physical disorders.

B   Exposure to an identified psychosocial stressor (e.g. bereavement, trauma, abuse, other life events and transitions) has resulted in the reaction of loss of appetite, **over a three-month period**.

C   Weight loss has been significant over **at least the previous three months**. This should preferably be confirmed by weight measurement.

Note 1: The term psychogenic loss of appetite disorder, currently in episode [IIIB6.6i]; [–]; [–] should be used (in place of psychogenic loss of appetite episode) if the person has experienced a previous DC–LD psychogenic loss of appetite episode.

Note 2: The term psychogenic loss of appetite disorder, currently in remission [IIIB6.6ii]; [–]; [–] should be used (in place of psychogenic loss of appetite episode) if the person is currently in remission, but has experienced at least two previous DC–LD psychogenic loss of appetite episodes.

IIIB6.7   Food faddiness/food refusal disorder

A   The symptoms/signs are not a direct consequence of other psychiatric disorders (e.g. pervasive developmental disorder, depressive episode, anorexia nervosa), drugs, or physical disorders.

B   Repeated failure to eat an adequate or balanced dietary intake (owing to refusal of food and/or extreme faddiness) **at least daily**, when this is presented by reasonably competent caregivers.

C   Failure to gain weight, or loss of weight, has been present **over at least the previous three months**. This should be confirmed by weight measurement.

IIIB6.8   Food rumination/regurgitation disorder

A   The symptoms/signs are not a direct consequence of other psychiatric disorders (e.g. depressive episode, manic episode, anorexia nervosa, bulimia nervosa), drugs or physical disorders.

B   Repeated food regurgitation (i.e. bringing swallowed food back up into the mouth) *and/ or* food rumination (i.e. re-chewing swallowed food) occurs **at least daily** when an adequate and balanced diet is presented by reasonably competent caregivers.

C   Failure to gain weight, or loss of weight, has been present over **at least the previous three months**. This should be confirmed by weight measurement.

IIIB6.9   Pica

A   The symptoms/signs are not a direct consequence of other psychiatric disorders (e.g. depressive episode, anorexia nervosa, bulimia nervosa) or physical disorder (e.g. iron deficiency).

B   Pica has occurred **at least twice a week over at least the previous three months**.

C   The pica must have the following characteristics:
   1   Repeated eating *and/or* mouthing of non-nutritive substances, for example, soil, paper, paint chippings, soap, hair, dust, fabric, cigarette stubs, faeces, discarded raw or frozen foods
   2   Out of keeping with the person's cultural background.

IIIB6.10   Excessive chewing/spitting out food disorder

A   The symptoms/signs are not a direct consequence of other psychiatric disorders (e.g. anorexia nervosa, obsessive–compulsive disorder) or physical disorder (e.g. dysphagia).

B   Repeated excessive chewing *and/or* spitting out without swallowing occurs **at least daily**, when an adequate and balanced diet is presented by reasonably competent caregivers.

C   Failure to gain weight, or loss of weight, has been present **over at least the previous three months**. This should be confirmed by weight measurements.

Hyperkinetic disorders: Introduction

DC–LD includes the following disorders in this group:

- IIIB7.1   Attention-deficit hyperactivity disorder of adults (childhood onset) [equivalent to F90.0, F7*x*.13]; [equivalent to 314.01]
- IIIB7.2   Attention-deficit hyperactivity disorder of adults (age of onset unknown) [equivalent to F90.0, F7*x*.13]; [equivalent to 314.01]

Attention-deficit hyperactivity disorder of adults (ADHD) usually presents early in life, typically in the first five years. The disorder is characterised by a pattern of impulsive, overactive, and poorly organised behaviour, in the context of a marked inability to maintain attention, and lack of purposeful and organised task-centred behaviour. Poor sleep may also be a feature. These features persist across different situations, and longitudinally over time. In the general population, it has been estimated that persistence into adulthood may occur in as many as 50–80% of cases, although ADHD of childhood is commonly succeeded in adulthood by a personality disorder without any marked attention deficit. In adults with learning disabilities, these latter cases should be categorised according to the prevailing picture in adulthood, not as ADHD.

   In adults with learning disabilities, the disorder may be easily overlooked, because the combination of poor attention, impulsive, disorganised behaviour and difficulty in initiating and maintaining purposeful behaviour is common among people with learning disabilities. The diagnosis is only to be applied where the overall picture is in excess of that which might be expected on the basis of general intelligence, or severity of learning disabilities. When the typical picture presents in adults with learning disabilities but its origin is known definitely *not* to have been early in life, ADHD should not be diagnosed: other diagnoses should be sought and considered. When adults with learning disabilities present with the typical picture of ADHD, but no early developmental history is available (owing to loss of contact with or bereavement of parents and no alternative source of background information), the second of the two diagnostic categories should be used.

Comorbidity is common. Adults with learning disabilities who have additional ADHD may also present with pervasive developmental disorders and other major psychiatric disorders. These should be coded separately. However, in keeping with the general approach of DC–LD, a hierarchical approach should be employed, such that, where any present-ing pattern of poor attention and disorganised behaviour that appears to amount to a potential diagnosis of ADHD is explainable on the basis of – for example – a manic episode, the category of ADHD is not ascribed. However, in exploring such possibilities, it is important to maintain a developmental perspective. So for anyone in whom ADHD has been present from early in life, any additional psychiatric disorder of adulthood should be recorded separately. In the above example, a manic episode might be ascribed, if appropriate.

IIIB7.1   Attention-deficit hyperactivity disorder of adults (childhood onset)

A   The symptoms must have had onset before the age of seven years.

B   Symptoms must not be a direct consequence of other psychiatric disorders (e.g. dementia, delirium, manic episode), drugs or physical disorders, for example hyperthyroidism.

C   The person has a pattern of inattention and distractibility, with poor concentration, flitting and fleeting activity (rapidly changing patterns of motor activity), lack of sustained purposeful action, and interruption of purposeful tasks, which is *not* accounted for by general intelligence or severity of learning disabilities.

D   Affected adults act impatiently and impulsively, with
    undue care and attention to consequences for themselves
    and others, to an extent that is *not* accounted for by
    general intelligence or severity of learning disabilities.

E   Motor over-activity, restlessness, and a marked inability to
    keep still are present, often most noticeable when
    affected individuals are seated.

F   The disorder is both pervasive across different situations
    and persistent longitudinally over time.

IIIB7.2   Attention-deficit hyperactivity disorder of adults (age of onset unknown)

A   The age of onset of the disorder is unknown, owing to
    lack of any available written early developmental history
    and lack of any possible informant history regarding early
    development. However, the disorder is known to
    long-standing, extending back as far as the available
    history.

B   Symptoms must not be a direct consequence of other
    psychiatric disorders (e.g. dementia, delirium, manic
    episode), drugs or physical disorders, for example
    hyperthyroidism.

C   The person has a pattern of inattention and distractibility,
    with poor concentration, flitting and fleeting activity
    (rapidly changing patterns of motor activity), lack of
    sustained purposeful action, and interruption of
    purposeful tasks, which is *not* accounted for by general
    intelligence or level of learning disabilities.

D   Affected adults act impatiently and impulsively, with
    undue care and attention to consequences for themselves
    and others, to an extent that is *not* accounted for by
    general intelligence or level of learning disabilities.

E   Motor over-activity, restlessness, and a marked inability to
    keep still are present, often most noticeable when
    affected individuals are seated.

F   The disorder is both pervasive across different situations
    and persists longitudinally over time.

Tic and movement disorders: Introduction

Tic disorders are included within the 'disorders of childhood and adolescence' section of ICD–10. These disorders can occur in adults with learning disabilities, most usually persisting from childhood or adolescent onset. Please note that organic movement disorders are also listed within ICD–10 chapter VI (diseases of the nervous system), including: hereditary ataxia; secondary parkinsonism; dystonia; and extrapyramidal and movement disorders, unspecified. The ICD–10 manuals should be consulted for details of diagnostic criteria if use of the categories listed below is considered:

* Transient tic disorder [F95.0]; [equivalent to 307.21]
* Chronic motor or vocal tic disorder [F95.1]; [equivalent to 307.22]
* Combined vocal and multiple motor tic disorder (Tourette's syndrome) [F95.2]; [equivalent to 307.23]
* Other tic disorders [F95.8]; [equivalent to 307.20]
* Tic disorder, unspecified [F95.9]; [–]
* Stereotyped movement disorders [F98.4]; [equivalent to 307.3]

DC–LD LEVEL C: PERSONALITY DISORDERS

Personality disorders: Introduction

DC–LD includes the following disorders in this group:

* IIIC1.1   Personality disorder, unspecified [equivalent to F60.9]; [–]
* IIIC1.2   Paranoid personality disorder [equivalent to F60.0]; [equivalent to 301.0]
* IIIC1.3   Dissocial personality disorder [equivalent to F60.2]; [equivalent to 301.7]
* IIIC1.4   Emotionally unstable personality disorder – impulsive type [equivalent to F60.30]; [equivalent to 301.9]
* IIIC1.5   Emotionally unstable personality disorder – borderline type [equivalent to F60.31]; [equivalent to 301.83]
* IIIC1.6   Histrionic personality disorder [equivalent to F60.4]; [equivalent to 301.50]
* IIIC1.7   Anankastic personality disorder [equivalent to F60.5]; [equivalent to 301.4]

- IIIC1.8   Other specific personality disorder [equivalent to F60.8]; [equivalent to 301.81, 301.9]
- Other ICD–10 personality disorders

The term 'personality disorder' is that used in the ICD–10 manuals. There are debates about the nosological status of personality disorders, and some controversy as to whether it is appropriate to use the term 'disorder' when describing patterns of personality characteristics that persist over time. The dividing line between 'disorder' or accepted normality is made on the basis of the severity/intensity of characteristics/ traits, rather than psychopathological abnormalities of form (such as delusions and hallucinations). As such the dividing line may be considered arbitrary. An additional consideration with people with learning disabilities is their developmental delay, that is, at what stage may the development of personality be considered as complete? To an extent, this issue is also relevant for the general population, as personality continues to develop throughout life and may be influenced in a lasting way by positive, nurturing, insightful experiences or negative, damaging experiences during adulthood. However, lasting personality characteristics of people of average ability develop by adolescence. The developmental phase for personality characteristics among people with learning disabilities should be viewed as longer than that for a person of average ability.

The purpose of diagnostic classification is to provide a meaningful shorthand description of a cluster of psychopathological items, which is used to inform the development of effective treatment/care plans and provides some expectation/knowledge of likely outcomes and prognosis, enabling long-term planning of support and care. The existing knowledge of personality disorders among adults with learning disabilities suggests that their diagnosis provides a short-term description, some indication as to longer-term prognosis and may start to guide care plans. As such, the category is retained within DC–LD. However, it must be acknowledged that previous studies reporting high rates of personality disorders in adults with learning disabilities have adopted various diagnostic approaches and classifications, with no consistency about the utility of the differing categories in clinical and research work. Further research to establish the utility, epidemiology, aetiology, biology, psychological and social comorbidity, natural history, and, most importantly, the appropriate management and outcomes of personality disorders is required. The use of the consensus criteria within this section of DC–LD could support such research. If consensus diagnostic criteria are not employed, it will remain difficult to compare clinical practice, service and research findings regarding adults with learning disabilities and personality disorders across different clinical populations, research samples, service and legal settings.

The ICD–10 manuals adopt inconsistent hierarchical diagnostic approaches to the classification of personality disorders, which DC–LD has aimed to address. The ICD–10 criteria provided for organic personality disorder are likely to lead to its over-diagnosis: use of this category purely on the grounds of the person having learning disabilities, a learning disabilities syndrome with an associated behavioural pheno-type, or epilepsy is not recommended (as discussed in the section 'ICD–10 'organic' disorders'). The ICD–10 suggestion that diagnosis can be made by the age of 16–17 years is viewed as too young for such a diagnosis in a person with learning disabilities. A higher threshold (over 21 years) is considered more clinically appropriate. There are obvious differential diagnostic difficulties with some ICD–10 person-ality disorder subtypes, owing to the need to distinguish from Axes I and III Level A disorders, that is, schizoid, dependent and anxious (avoidant) personality disorders. Hence, DC–LD recommends that these categories are not usually used. Personality disorders should only be diagnosed when the identified characteristics cannot be explained by identified disorders in Axes I, II, III Level A or B, or by physical disorder (which may be recorded using Appendix 2).

It is unlikely that personality disorders could be diagnosed in adults with severe/profound learning dis-abilities; however, diagnosis is appropriate for some adults with mild/moderate learning disabilities. Axis III Level C diagnostic criteria have not primarily been developed for use with adults with learning disabilities who offend, although this group includes people with personality disorder who commit infrequent 'high-impact' offences. Other descriptive approaches need to be developed for this special group, to be used alongside the DC–LD.

Personality disorders are severe disturbances in the characterological constitution and behavioural traits of an individual, involving several areas of his or her personality.

They are associated with considerable personal and social disruption to the individual him- or herself and/or others. The diagnostic criteria for personality disorders, unspecified should be used to determine whether or not the adult has a personality disorder. Where these criteria are met, further sub-classification as a specific personality disorder subtype should be considered, that is, into one of paranoid, dissocial, emotionally unstable, histrionic, or anankastic personality disorder. The category 'other specific personality disorder' should be used where the general diagnostic criteria are met, but when none of the six subtypes described above are appropriate. The ICD–10 categories of 'schizoid', 'anxious (avoidant)' and 'dependent' personality disorders should usually be avoided in view of the difficulty in differentiating from the underlying learning disabilities. It is unlikely that more than one personality disorder subtype would be diagnosed in the same individual.

IIIC1.1   Personality disorder, unspecified

A   Characteristics/traits include markedly disharmonious attitudes and behaviour from those which are culturally expected and accepted. Several areas of functioning are involved, such as: affectivity; emotional control; arousal; impulse-control; outlook, interpreting and thinking; and style of relating to others.

B   The characteristics/traits must not be a direct consequence of the person's severity of learning disabilities, pervasive developmental disorders, other psychiatric illness, drugs or physical disorders.

C   The characteristics/traits are apparent by adolescence and continue into adulthood and represent a continuous developmental trajectory from the time they were first identifiable.

D   The characteristics/traits are chronic, pervasive and maladaptive across a broad range of personal and social situations.

E   The characteristics/traits lead to considerable personal distress for the individual and/or others, although this may not become apparent until late in the course of the personality disorder.

F   There are associated significant problems in occupational and/or social functioning.

G   The person is **at least 21 years of age**.

IIIC1.2   Paranoid personality disorder

A   The criteria for personality disorder, unspecified must be met.

B   At least four of the following must be present:
1   Excessive sensitivity to setbacks and rebuffs
2   Tendency to bear grudges persistently
3   Suspiciousness and a pervasive tendency to distort experiences by misconstruing the neutral or friendly actions of others as hostile or contemptuous
4   A combative or tenacious sense of personal rights out-of-keeping with the actual situation
5   Persistent self-referential attitude, associated with self-importance
6   Preoccupation with unsubstantiated conspiratorial explanations of events
7   Recurrent unjustified suspicions about the sexual fidelity of the person's partner.

IIIC1.3   Dissocial personality disorder

A   The criteria for personality disorder, unspecified must be met.

B   At least three of the following must be present:
1   Callous unconcern for the feelings of others
2   Gross and persistent irresponsibility and disregard for social norms, rules and obligations
3   Incapacity to maintain enduring relationships, though no difficulty in establishing them
4   Very low tolerance to frustration and a low threshold for discharge of aggression, including violence
5   Incapacity to experience guilt, or to profit from adverse experience
6   Marked proneness to blame others, or to offer plausible rationalisations for the behaviour that has brought the individual into conflict with society.

IIIC1.4 Emotionally unstable personality disorder – impulsive type

A The criteria for personality disorder, unspecified must be met.

B The person must demonstrate a marked tendency to quarrelsome behaviour and to conflict with others, especially when impulsive acts are thwarted or criticised.

C At least two of the following must be present:
1 Marked tendency to act unexpectedly and without consideration of the consequences
2 Liability to outbursts of anger or violence, with inability to control the resulting behavioural explosions
3 Difficulty in maintaining any course of action that offers no immediate reward
4 Unstable and capricious mood.

IIIC1.5 Emotionally unstable personality disorder – borderline type

A The criteria for personality disorder, unspecified must be met.

B At least three of the following must be present:
1 Marked tendency to quarrelsome behaviour and to conflict with others, especially when impulsive acts are thwarted or criticised
2 Marked tendency to act unexpectedly and without consideration of the consequences
3 Liability to outbursts of anger or violence, with inability to control the resulting behavioural explosions
4 Difficulty in maintaining any course of action that offers no immediate reward
5 Unstable and capricious mood.

C At least two of the following must be present:
1 Disturbances in and uncertainty about self-image, aims, and internal preferences (including sexual)
2 Liability to become involved in intense and unstable relationships, often leading to emotional crises

3   Excessive efforts to avoid abandonment
4   Recurrent threats or acts of self-harm
5   Chronic feelings of emptiness.

IIIC1.6   Histrionic personality disorder

A   The criteria for personality disorder, unspecified must be met.

B   At least four of the following must be present:
1   Self-dramatisation, theatricality, or exaggerated expression of emotions
2   Suggestibility
3   Shallow and labile affectivity
4   Continual seeking for excitement and activities in which the individual is the centre of attention
5   Inappropriate seductiveness in appearance or behaviour
6   Over-concern with physical attractiveness.

IIIC1.7   Anankastic personality disorder

A   The criteria for personality disorder, unspecified must be present.

B   At least four of the following must be met:
1   Feelings of excessive doubt and caution
2   Preoccupation with details, rules, lists, order, organisation or schedule
3   Perfectionism that interferes with task completion
4   Excessive conscientiousness and scrupulousness
5   Undue preoccupation with productivity to the exclusion of pleasure and interpersonal relationships
6   Excessive pedantry and adherence to social conventions
7   Rigidity and stubbornness
8   Unreasonable insistence by the individual that others submit to exactly his or her way of doing things, or unreasonable reluctance to allow others to do things.

IIIC1.8   Other specific personality disorder

This category can be used to describe specific disorders not currently included in DC–LD or ICD–10.

Other ICD–10 personality disorders

The following ICD–10 personality disorders may be relevant in certain situations, for example personality change secondary to leucotomy. Please note that this category should *not* be used purely because the person with personality problems has learning disabilities, has epilepsy, or because there is an underlying cause for his or her learning disabilities that is associated with a behavioural phenotype that includes personality problems (as described more fully in the section headed 'ICD–10 'organic' disorders'). The ICD–10 manuals should be consulted for details of diagnostic criteria if use of this category is considered:

- Organic personality disorder [F07.0]; [equivalent to 310.1]

Other types of personality disorders are included in ICD–10. The ICD–10 manuals should be consulted for details of diagnostic criteria if use of these categories is considered:

- Schizoid personality disorder [F60.1]; [equivalent to 301.20]
- Anxious (avoidant) personality disorder [F60.6]; [equivalent to 301.82]
- Dependent personality disorder [F60.7]; [equivalent to 301.6]

DC–LD LEVEL D: PROBLEM BEHAVIOURS

Problem behaviours: Introduction

DC–LD includes the following behaviours in this group:
- IIID1.1   General diagnostic criteria for problem behaviours [equivalent to F7*x*.1, F69]; [–]
- IIID1.2   Verbally aggressive behaviour [equivalent to F7*x*.1, F68.8]; [equivalent to 312.9]
- IIID1.3   Physically aggressive behaviour [equivalent to F7*x*.15, F68.8]; [equivalent to 312.9]
- IIID1.4   Destructive behaviour [equivalent to F7*x*.1, F68.8]; [equivalent to 312.9]
- IIID1.5   Self-injurious behaviour [equivalent to F7*x*.11, F68.8]; [equivalent to 312.9]

- IIID1.6 Sexually inappropriate behaviour [equivalent to F7*x*.1, F68.8]; [equivalent to 312.9]
- IIID1.7 Oppositional behaviour [equivalent to F7*x*.1, F91.3, F68.8]; [equivalent to 313.81, 312.9]
- IIID1.8 Demanding behaviour [equivalent to F7*x*.1, F68.8]; [equivalent to 312.9]
- IIID1.9 Wandering behaviour [equivalent to F7*x*.14, F68.8]; [equivalent to 312.9]
- IIID1.10(*x*–*x*) Mixed problem behaviours [equivalent to F7*x*.1, F68.8]; [equivalent to 312.9]
- IIID1.11 Other problem behaviours [equivalent to F7*x*.1, F68.8]; [equivalent to 312.9]
- IIID1.12 Mixed other problem behaviours [equivalent to F7*x*.1, F68.8]; [equivalent to 312.9]

There are debates about the nosological status of problem behaviours, and controversy as to whether or not the term 'behaviour disorders' should be used when describing long-standing patterns of problem behaviour. Within DC–LD, the term 'problem behaviours' is employed for these descriptive categories. The category is included in DC–LD in view of their high prevalence among adults with learning disabilities, and in recognition that, when present, the provision of appropriate professional assessment leading to development of individualised treatment/support care plans is essential. Failure of a classificatory system to recognise that such needs may occur and require professional input is viewed as unhelpful to those adults with identified needs falling within these categories. In using these terms, there are no implied assumptions as to the aetiology or long-term prognosis of the problem behaviours. Within the UK and Republic of Ireland, adults with learning disabilities and problem behaviours are often referred to specialist learning disabilities health services for multi-professional assessment, from which the treatment/support care plans are devised in an individualised way. This requires the assessment of mental health, physical health and psychological needs, and environmental, sociocultural, communication and service issues, which may all be contributory to the presentation of problem behaviours. In order to determine whether specialised interventions are required, and whether it is appropriate to use a descriptive category from Axis III Level D, the health professional will need to consider the function, frequency, severity and chronicity of the behaviour, its impact on the person's quality of life, and associated risks to the person him- or herself and/or others.

The main Axis III Level D problem behaviour categories should only be ascribed when the identified behaviour is *not* a direct consequence of pervasive developmental disorder, psychiatric illness, personality disorder or physical illness. Those psychiatrists who wish to refer to such situations should use the supplementary categories (described later in this level) that specifically state the underlying cause of the problem behaviour. This would include the example of a person with autism who is severely physically aggressive to other people as a *direct consequence* of his or her autism (i.e. through the distress/anxiety associated with interruption of a ritual). Axis III Level D problem behaviours may also coexist in a person with disorders on other axes. For example, a person with long-standing self-injurious behaviour may develop a superimposed depressive episode: in this case both the Axis III Level B disorder and Axis III Level D behaviour should be recorded. In this example, should the long-standing self-injurious behaviour increase in severity and/or frequency at the time of the depressive episode, then both the Axis III Level B disorder and the Axis III Level D behaviour should still be recorded. If the person *only* experiences self-injurious behaviour at the time of his or her depressive episode, then only his or her Axis III Level B disorder (depressive episode) should be recorded, or alternatively the depressive episode should be recorded together with the supplementary criteria 'problem behaviour due to psychiatric illness (self-injurious behaviour)'.

With regard to behavioural phenotypes, diagnostic approaches have been discussed in the sections 'Behavioural phenotypes' and 'A hierarchical approach to diagnosis'. Where a problem behaviour is an essential and integral part of the diagnostic criteria for the clinical syndrome to be diagnosed, then a separate record of an Axis III Level D problem behaviour should *not* be made. Where the learning disabilities syndrome is diagnosed on the basis of genetic testing, or on clinical criteria that do not rely upon the presence of the problem behaviour, then when the problem behaviour associated with the syndrome *is* present, this *should be* separately recorded as an Axis III Level D problem behaviour.

Many problem behaviours that are minor problems of brief duration occur as an understandable response to environmental stressors or situations (in which case, they may meet criteria for adjustment disorder), or have communicative or other functions. Such cases should *not* be recorded as Axis III Level D behaviours. The dividing line between such minor problems and the presence of an Axis III Level D problem behaviour could be considered as arbitrary. However, without consensus-agreed criteria, it would remain difficult to high-light clinical needs or to compare clinical practice, service, and research findings regarding adults with learning disabilities across different clinical populations and research samples, service and legal settings. Further research to establish the utility, epidemiology, aetiology, biological, psychological and social comorbidity, natural history, appropriate management and outcomes of problem behaviours is required. The consensus criteria in DC–LD could be used to support such work.

The ICD–10 manuals adopt inconsistent hierarchical approaches to the classification of problem behaviours. Within the ICD–10 coding of severity of mental retardation, additional code numbers are allowed to indicate the associated degree of impairment of behaviour (none, minimal or clinically significant), and certain types of behaviour are specified in the ICD–10–MR. However, this approach is out of keeping with the consensus of UK and Republic of Ireland clinical practice, where a hierarchical approach is adopted. Additionally, some of the behaviours that ICD–10 codes in this way are viewed by DC–LD as being better recorded elsewhere, for example pica and hyperkinesis. It is recommended that the ICD–10 category of organic behaviour disorders (F07.8) is avoided, in view of its assumptions regarding aetiology, for the reasons previously stated in the section 'ICD–10 'organic' disorders'. ICD–10 itself codes some behaviours in more than one category, for example hair-pulling (F7*x*.16) versus trichotillomania (F63.3), and hyperkinesis (F7*x*.13) versus hyperkinetic disorder (F90). Some more prevalent maladaptive behaviours are not included within ICD–10, for example, destructiveness. DC–LD therefore deviates from ICD–10 in the approaches taken within Axis III Level D. Within DC–LD, pica is grouped together with other eating disorders on Axis III Level B. The ICD–10 and DSM–IV codes that clinicians may consider to correspond to the DC–LD problem behaviours, in whole or in part, include those listed in parentheses at the beginning of this introduction.

Axis III Level D has not primarily been developed for use with adults with learning disabilities who offend, although some people with recordable Axis III Level D problem behaviours may commit infrequent 'high-impact' offences. Other descriptive approaches need to be developed for this special group, to be used alongside DC–LD.

The general diagnostic criteria for problem behaviours should be used to determine whether or not the adult has a recordable problem behaviour. Where these criteria are met, the problem behaviour should be sub-classified into: verbally aggressive behaviour, physically aggressive behaviour, destructive behaviour, self-injurious behaviour, sexually inappropriate behaviour, oppositional behaviour, demanding behaviour, or wandering behaviour. Sometimes, more than one, or several, types of Axis III Level D problem behaviours should be recorded for the same individual. The category 'other problem behaviour' should be used where the general diagnostic criteria are met, but when none of the subtypes described above are appropriate. The category 'mixed problem behaviour' should be used when more than one specific problem behaviour is present (the specific problem behaviours should additionally be listed), whereas the category 'other mixed problem behaviour' should be used when the general diagnostic criteria are met for two or more behaviours that are not described by the specific subtypes.

In some circumstances, problem behaviours may be reduced in frequency or severity by the use of long-term ongoing interventions/supports or external environmental manipulations that reduce opportunity for the problem behaviour. In such circumstances, it would be expected that withdrawal of these protective packages would have negative consequences for the individual in terms of increase in problem behaviours and the sequelae of these. In these cases, clinical judgement should be used as to whether the term problem behaviour and specification of its type should be used, even though item B of the criteria for the type of problem behaviour is not met.

IIID1.1   General diagnostic criteria for problem behaviours

A   The problem behaviour is of significant frequency, severity or chronicity as to require clinical assessment and special interventions/support.

B   The problem behaviour must not be a direct consequence of other psychiatric disorders (e.g. pervasive developmental disorders, non-affective psychotic disorders, depressive episode, generalised anxiety disorders, obsessive–compulsive disorder, personality disorders), drugs or physical disorders.

C   One of the following must be present:
1   The problem behaviour results in a significant negative impact on the person's quality of life or the quality of life of others. This may be owing to restriction of his or her lifestyle, social opportunities, independence, community integration, service access or choices, or adaptive functioning
2   The problem behaviour presents significant risks to the health and/or safety of the person and/or others.

D   The problem behaviour is persistent and pervasive. It is present across a range of personal and social situations, although may be more severe in certain identified settings.

IIID1.2   Verbally aggressive behaviour

A   General diagnostic criteria for problem behaviour are met.

B   Verbal aggression must have occurred **on at least three occasions in the preceding six-month period**, for example the person uses his or her voice in a violent or threatening manner. This may be impulsive or planned, and must occur in the context of minimal or no provocation by others.

IIID1.3   Physically aggressive behaviour

A   General diagnostic criteria for problem behaviour are met.

B   Physical aggression must have occurred **on at least three occasions in the preceding six-month period**, for example the person uses or threatens physical violence. This may be impulsive or planned, and occurs in the context of minimal or no provocation by others. Severity may range from pushing, slapping, and physically intimidating, to punching, kicking, biting, pulling the hair of others and more serious physical assault.

IIID1.4   Destructive behaviour

A   General diagnostic criteria for problem behaviour are met.

B   Destructive behaviour must have occurred **on at least three occasions in the preceding six-month period**, for example the person damages property, such as tearing paper and fabrics, smashing furniture and glass, to more serious property damage and fire setting. This may be impulsive or planned, and occurs in the context of minimal or no provocation by others.

IIID1.5   Self-injurious behaviour

A   General diagnostic criteria for problem behaviour are met.

B   Self-injury sufficient to cause tissue damage, such as bruising, scarring, tissue loss and dysfunction, must have occurred **during most weeks of the preceding six-month period**, for example ranging from skin-picking/scratching, hair-pulling, face-tapping/slapping to biting hands, lips, and other body parts, rectal/genital-poking, eye-poking and head-banging.

C   The self-injurious behaviour is not a deliberate suicide attempt.

IIID1.6   Sexually inappropriate behaviour

A   General diagnostic criteria for problem behaviour are met.

B   Sexually inappropriate behaviour must have occurred **on at least three occasions in the preceding six-month period**, for example ranging from the person touching, fondling, kissing another person/other people in a way that is unwelcome and/or offensive, to obscene communications, genital exposure, public masturbation and sexual assault. This may be impulsive or planned and includes sexually inappropriate behaviour resulting from under-development of social skills, lack of sexual education, misinterpretation of a relationship and sexual frustration.

IIID1.7   Oppositional behaviour

A   General diagnostic criteria for problem behaviour are met.

B   Oppositional behaviour must have occurred **at least weekly over the preceding six-month period**, for example persistent, defiant and uncooperative behaviours ranging from defying rules and requests to refusing to move or socially engage/disengage (despite being able to do so) to more disruptive behaviour such as lying in the road. This behaviour occurs in the context of minimal or no provocation by others.

IIID1.8   Demanding behaviour

A   General diagnostic criteria for problem behaviour are met.

B   Demanding behaviours that are repeated, excessive, impatient and inappropriate given the needs of the adult with learning disabilities must have occurred **on at least most days over the preceding six-month period**, for example repeated requests, excessive clinging to others.

IIID1.9   Wandering behaviour

A   General diagnostic criteria for problem behaviour are met.

B   Wandering, darting or running away behaviours that place the person at some risk must have occurred **on at least three occasions in the preceding six-month period**. This may be impulsive or planned, and occur in the context of minimal or no provocation by others.

IIID1.10(*x–x*)   Mixed problem behaviours

A   More than one specific problem behaviour meeting the above diagnostic criteria is present.

> Note: This category should be used in conjunction with listing the types of specific problem behaviours, for example, mixed problem behaviour (verbally aggressive behaviour, physically aggressive behaviour, destructive behaviour) [IIID1.10 (2, 3, 4)].

IIID1.11   Other problem behaviours

A   General diagnostic criteria for problem behaviour are met.

B   A single specific problem behaviour, not individually classified by name in the categories listed above, must have occurred **on at least weekly occasions in the preceding six-month period**. Possible examples for coding within this category are: non-epileptic seizures; psychogenic polydipsia, spitting; playing with food; deliberate urinary or faecal incontinence, soiling and/or smearing; throwing objects; hoarding; stealing; begging; making hoax telephone calls; repeated lying; socially inappropriate behaviour etc.

IIID1.12 Mixed other problem behaviours

A   General diagnostic criteria for problem behaviour are met.

B   More than one specific problem behaviour, not individually classified by name in the categories listed above, must have occurred **on at least weekly occasions in the preceding six-month period**. Possible examples for coding within this category are: non-epileptic seizures; psychogenic polydipsia, spitting; playing with food; deliberate urinary or faecal incontinence, soiling and/or smearing; throwing objects; hoarding; stealing; begging; making hoax telephone calls; repeated lying; etc.

Supplementary categories – problem behaviours that are directly caused by other disorders: Introduction

For those psychiatrists who wish to use such categories, DC–LD provides supplementary criteria for problem behaviours that are directly caused by other disorders, as follows:

- IIID2.1(*x–x*)   Problem behaviour/s due to pervasive developmental disorder (specify type/s of problem behaviour/s) [–]; [–]
- IIID2.2(*x–x*)   Problem behaviour/s due to psychiatric illness (specify type/s of problem behaviour/s) [–]; [–]
- IIID2.3(*x–x*)   Problem behaviour/s due to personality disorder (specify type/s of problem behaviour/s) [–]; [–]
- IIID2.4(*x–x*)   Problem behaviour/s due to physical illness/disorder (specify type/s of problem behaviour/s) [–]; [–]

Use of these supplementary categories is optional. They should only be used when the cause of the problem behaviour is clear.

IIID2.1(*x–x*)   Problem behaviour/s due to pervasive developmental disorder (type/s)

A   The problem behaviour is of significant frequency or severity to require special interventions/support in addition to those for the pervasive developmental disorder.

B   The problem behaviour/s is/are a direct consequence of pervasive developmental disorder.

C   One of the following must be present:
1   The problem behaviour results in a significant negative impact on the person's quality of life or the quality of life of others. This may be owing to restriction of his or her lifestyle, social opportunities, independence, community integration, service access or choices, or adaptive functioning
2   The problem behaviour presents significant risks to the health and/or safety of the person and/or others.

D   The problem behaviour is persistent and pervasive. It is present across a range of personal and social situations, although it may be more severe in certain identified settings.

> Note: Specify the type/s of problem behaviour/s in brackets, for example problem behaviour due to pervasive developmental disorder (physically aggressive behaviour) [IIID2.1(3)].

IIID2.2(x–x)   Problem behaviour/s due to psychiatric illness (type/s)

A   The problem behaviour is of significant frequency or severity to require special interventions/support in addition to those for the psychiatric illness.

B   The problem behaviour/s is/are a direct consequence of psychiatric illness.

C   One of the following must be present:
1   The problem behaviour results in a significant negative impact on the person's quality of life or the quality of life of others. This may be owing to restriction of his or her lifestyle, social opportunities, independence, community integration, service access or choices, or adaptive functioning
2   The problem behaviour presents significant risks to the health and/or safety of the person and/or others.

D   The problem behaviour occurs during the course of the psychiatric illness. It is present across a range of personal and social situations, although it may be more severe in certain identified settings.

> Note: Specify the type/s of problem behaviour/s in brackets, for example problem behaviour due to psychiatric illness (physically aggressive behaviour) [IIID2.2(3)].

IIID2.3(*x–x*) Problem behaviour/s due to personality disorder (type/s)

A The problem behaviour is of significant frequency or severity to require special interventions/support in addition to those for the personality disorder.

B The problem behaviour/s is/are a direct consequence of personality disorder.

C One of the following must be present:
1 The problem behaviour results in a significant negative impact on the person's quality of life or the quality of life of others. This may be owing to restriction of his or her lifestyle, social opportunities, independence, community integration, service access or choices, or adaptive functioning
2 The problem behaviour presents significant risks to the health and/or safety of the person and/or others.

D The problem behaviour is persistent and pervasive. It is present across a range of personal and social situations, although it may be more severe in certain identified settings.

> Note: Specify the type/s of problem behaviour/s in brackets, for example problem behaviour due to personality disorder (physically aggressive behaviour) [IIID2.3(3)].

IIID2.4(*x–x*) Problem behaviour/s due to physical illness/disorder (type/s)

A The problem behaviour is of significant frequency or severity to require special interventions/support in addition to those for the physical illness/disorder.

B The problem behaviour/s is/are a direct consequence of physical illness/disorder.

C One of the following must be present:
1 The problem behaviour results in a significant negative impact on the person's quality of life or the quality of life of others. This may be owing to restriction of his or her lifestyle, social opportunities, independence, community integration, service access or choices, or adaptive functioning
2 The problem behaviour presents significant risks to the health and/or safety of the person and/or others.

D The problem behaviour occurs during the course of the physical illness/disorder. It is present across a range of personal and social situations, although it may be more severe in certain identified settings.

> Note: Specify the type/s of problem behaviour/s in brackets, for example problem behaviours due to physical illness/disorder (physically aggressive behaviour, self-injurious behaviour) [IIID2.4(3, 5)].

DC–LD Level E: Other disorders

Other disorders: Introduction

There are other groups of disorders included in ICD–10 that are not easily categorised within the framework of DC–LD Levels A–D; these disorders are listed below. The ICD–10 manuals should be consulted for details of diagnostic criteria if use of these categories is considered. With regard to sleep disorders, it should be noted that in addition to the non-organic sleep disorders that are grouped in ICD–10 chapter V (mental disorders), organic sleep disorders are categorised in ICD–10 chapter VI (diseases of the nervous system). A list of such disorders is outlined in Appendix 2. The category 'mental disorder, not otherwise specified' should only be used for those disorders that are not classifiable elsewhere within Axis III Levels A–E. In these circumstances, individual descriptions will be required.

• Mental and behavioural disorders due to use of alcohol [F10. *xx*]; [equivalent to 303.90, 305.00, 303.00, 291. *xx*]

- Mental and behavioural disorders due to use of opioids
  [F11. *xx*]; [equivalent to 304.00, 305.50, 292. *xx*]
- Mental and behavioural disorders due to use of
  cannabinoids [F12.*xx*]; [equivalent to 304.30, 305.20,
  292. *xx*]
- Mental and behavioural disorders due to use of sedatives
  or hypnotics [F13. *xx*]; [equivalent to 304.10, 305.40,
  292. *xx*]
- Mental and behavioural disorders due to use of cocaine
  [F14. *xx*]; [equivalent to 304.2, 305.6, 292. *xx*]
- Mental and behavioural disorders due to use of other
  stimulants, including caffeine [F15. *xx*]; [equivalent to
  304.40, 305.70, 305.90, 292. *xx*]
- Mental and behavioural disorders due to use of
  hallucinogens [F16. *xx*]; [304.50, 305.30, 292. *xx*]
- Mental and behavioural disorders due to use of tobacco
  [F17. *xx*]; [equivalent to 305.10, 292. *x*]
- Mental and behavioural disorders due to use of volatile
  solvents [F18. *xx*]; [equivalent to 304.60, 305.90, 292. *xx*]
- Mental and behavioural disorders due to use of multiple
  drug use and use of other psychoactive substances
  [F19. *xx*]; [equivalent to 304.90, 305.90, 292. *xx*, 304.80]

Within categories F10–F19, four or five character codes
may be used to specify the clinical condition:

- Acute intoxication [F1*x*.0]; [equivalent to 292.89]
- Harmful use [F1*x*.1]
- Dependence syndrome [F1*x*.2]
- Withdrawal state [F1*x*.3]; [equivalent to 292.0]
- Withdrawal state with delirium [F1*x*.4]; [equivalent to
  292.81]
- Psychotic disorder [F1*x*.5*x*]

.50	Schizophrenia-like [equivalent to 292.11, 292.12]	
.51	Predominantly delusional [equivalent to 292.11]	
.52	Predominantly hallucinatory [equivalent to 292.12]	
.53	Predominantly polymorphic [equivalent to 292.11, 292.12]	
.54	Predominantly depressive symptoms [equivalent to 292.84]	
.55	Predominantly manic symptoms [equivalent to 292.84]	
.56	Mixed [equivalent to 292.84]	

> Amnesic syndrome [F1*x*.6]; [equivalent to 291.1]
> Residual and late-onset psychotic disorder [F1*x*.7*x*]
>> .70   Flashbacks [equivalent to 292.89]
>> .71   Personality or behaviour disorder [–]
>> .72   Residual affective disorder [–]
>> .73   Dementia [equivalent to 291.2]
>> .74   Other persisting cognitive impairment [–]
>> .75   Late-onset psychotic disorder [–]
> Other mental and behavioural disorders [F1*x*.8]; [equivalent to 291.9]
> Unspecified mental and behavioural disorder [F1*x*.9]; [–]

- Non-organic sleep disorders
  > Non-organic insomnia [F51.0]; [equivalent to 307.42]
  > Non-organic hypersomnia [F51.1]; [equivalent to 307.44]
  > Non-organic disorder of the sleep–wake schedule [F51.2]; [equivalent to 307.45]
  > Sleepwalking (somnambulism) [F51.3]; [equivalent to 307.46]
  > Sleep terrors (night terrors) [F51.4]; [equivalent to 307.46]
  > Nightmares [F51.5]; [equivalent to 307.47]
  > Other non-organic sleep disorders [F51.8]; [equivalent to 307.47]
- Sexual dysfunction, not caused by organic disorder or disease [F52]; [equivalent to 302.7*x*, 306.51]
- Abuse of non-dependence-producing substances [F55]; [–]
- Habit and impulse disorders
  > Pathological gambling [F63.0]; [equivalent to 312.31]
  > Pathological stealing [F63.2]; [equivalent to 312.32]
  > Other habit and impulse disorders [F63.8]; [equivalent to 312.30]
  > Habit and impulse disorder, unspecified [F63.9]; [–]
- Gender identity disorders
  > Transsexualism [F64.0]; [equivalent to 302.85]
  > Dual-role transsexualism [F64.1]; [–]
  > Gender identity disorder of childhood [F64.2]; [equivalent to 302.6]
  > Other gender identity disorder [F64.8]; [equivalent to 302.6]
  > Gender identity disorder, unspecified [F64.9]; [–]

- Disorders of sexual preference
  - Fetishism [F65.0]; [equivalent to 302.81]
  - Fetishistic transvestism [F65.1]; [equivalent to 302.3]
  - Exhibitionism [F65.2]; [equivalent to 302.4]
  - Voyeurism [F65.3]; [equivalent to 302.82]
  - Paedophilia [F65.4]; [equivalent to 302.2]
  - Sadomasochism [F65.5]; [equivalent to 302.83, 302.84]
  - Multiple disorders of sexual preference [F65.6]; [equivalent to 302.9]
  - Other disorders of sexual preference [F65.8]; [equivalent to 302.89, 302.9]
  - Disorder of sexual preference, unspecified [F65.9]; [–]
- Psychological and behavioural disorders associated with sexual development and orientation
  - Sexual maturation disorder [F66.0]; [equivalent to 302.9]
  - Egodystonic sexual orientation [F66.1]; [equivalent to 302.9]
  - Sexual relationship disorder [F66.2]; [equivalent to 302.9]
  - Other psychosexual developmental disorders [F66.8]; [equivalent to 302.9]
  - Psychosexual developmental disorder, unspecified [F66.9]; [equivalent to 302.9]
- Mental disorder, not otherwise specified [F99]; [equivalent to 300.9]

ACKNOWLEDGEMENTS

Secretarial support for the development of DC–LD was provided by Mrs Jean Davis and Mrs Gill Green of Rockingham Forest NHS Trust, Northamptonshire. The DC–LD working group was convened on behalf of The Penrose Society, while Dr Richard Collacott was its President, and the Faculty for the Psychiatry of Learning Disability of The Royal College of Psychiatrists, while Dr Mary Lindsey was its Chair.

Financial support for publication of this volume was received from the Faculty for the Psychiatry of Learning Disability of The Royal College of Psychiatrists.

REFERENCES

AMERICAN PSYCHIATRIC ASSOCIATION (1994) *Diagnostic and Statistical Manual of Mental Disorders.* Fourth edition. Washington, DC: APA.

HACHINSKI, V. C., ILIFF, L. D., ZILHKA, E., *ET AL* (1975) Cerebral blood flow in dementia. *Archives of Neurology, 32,* 632–637.

HOLM, V. A., CASSIDY, S. B., BUTLER, M. G., *ET AL* (1993) Prader-Willi syndrome. Consensus diagnostic criteria. *Pediatrics, 91,* 398–402.

SPARROW, S. S., BALLA, D. A. & CICCHETTI, D. V. (1984) *Vineland Adaptive Behaviour Scales: A Revision of the Vineland Social Maturity Scale by Edgar A. Doll.* Circle-Pines, Minnesota: American Guidance Service.

WORLD HEALTH ORGANIZATION (1992) *ICD–10 Classification of Mental and Behavioural Disorders – Clinical Description and Diagnostic Guidelines.* ICD–10–CDDG. Geneva: WHO.

—— (1993) *ICD–10 Classification of Mental and Behavioural Disorders – Diagnostic Criteria for Research.* ICD–10–DCR. Geneva: WHO.

—— (1996) *ICD–10 Guide for Mental Retardation.* ICD–10–MR. Geneva: WHO.

APPENDIX 1: LEARNING DISABILITIES SYNDROMES AND BEHAVIOURAL PHENOTYPES

Several of the disorders contained within Axis II of DC–LD are associated with a characteristic behavioural phenotype. As previously discussed under the sub-sections 'ICD–10 'organic' disorders' and 'A hierarchical approach to diagnosis', any symptoms/traits that *are necessary* clinical features in order to make the diagnosis of the learning disabilities syndrome (Axis II disorder) should *not* be recorded as a separate disorder in Axes III Levels B–E (e.g. the over-eating of Prader-Willi syndrome). Conversely, symptoms/traits that are considered to be associated with the syndrome (part of the behavioural phenotype) but which *are not* essential clinical features of the learning disabilities syndrome (Axis II disorder) should be recorded as separate disorders in Axis III Levels B–E (e.g. dementia in a person with Down's syndrome). Psychiatric illnesses that are a recognised feature of the syndrome's behavioural phenotype should be recorded under the relevant heading in Axis III in preference to following the assumptions made within the ICD–10 categories of organic disorders (as previously discussed).

There follows short descriptions of the behavioural phenotypes of some learning disabilities syndromes:

Aicardi syndrome

Aicardi syndrome is an X-linked dominant disorder that manifests only in girls, being lethal in male conceptuses. Diagnosis relies on agenesis of the corpus callosum, severe epilepsy (infantile spasms/hypsarrhythmia), and typical choroidoretinal lacunae. It commonly results in severe disabilities, lethargy, self-injury, aggression and frequent night wakening.

Angelman syndrome

Angelman syndrome is a mostly sporadic, non-familial congenital disorder affecting about 1 in 12 000 children. It results in severe learning disabilities and inappropriate bouts of laughter and a jerky, ataxic pattern of movement and gait. Much recent work has focused on the characteristically cheerful and excitable temperament most individuals display and also on expressive language delay and deviance, in the context of comparatively preserved receptive skills. A typical feature of the condition is 'insistence on sameness', and there is a corresponding high rate of autistic behaviours.

Cornelia de Lange syndrome

Cornelia de Lange syndrome is a rare disorder (estimated around 1 in 40 000 to 100 000), which was previously also known as Amsterdam Dwarfism. Its cause is unknown: the condition is not usually familial. There is a typical facial appearance with a small upturned nose, anteverted nostrils, and prominent, well-defined eyebrows that fan out laterally as well as meeting together. With age, the eyebrows typically become bushy, and the nose and lips more prominent. Psychological research has concentrated on language function, including guttural tone of vocal expression, the occurrence of autistic-type features, and self-stimulatory behaviour, often of a self-injurious nature.

Cri du Chat syndrome

Cri du chat syndrome is a rare condition occurring in approximately 1 per 50 000 live births. It is due to a partial deletion of chromosome 5. Most cases are *de novo* deletions. There is a great deal of cytogenetic heterogeneity, with the more severe phenotype associated with translocations. General delay is invariable, with poor weight gain. Many individuals never learn to walk. The person's learning disabilities are usually severe, but there have been some reports of mild to moderate learning disabilities. Most individuals are placid, but hyperactivity and restless irritability, with self-stimulatory and destructive behaviour is not uncommon.

Down's syndrome

Down's syndrome is the commonest genetic syndrome causing learning disabilities, with an overall natural occurrence of 1 in 600 live births. Its occurrence increases with increasing maternal age, ranging from 1 in 2500 at maternal age under 30 years, rising to 1 in 32 at maternal age over 45 years. Three genetic subtypes of this trisomy (21) syndrome are recognised: 95% are non-familial, sporadic cases arising from non-dysjunction; up to 5% are translocations between, usually, chromosomes 14 and 21; 1–2% are mosaics, where both trisomy 21 and normal cell lines occur in the same individual. This latter variant usually results in a lesser degree of learning disabilities. This condition has been much-studied, especially concerning the occurrence of dementia in Alzheimer's disease in middle-aged and elderly subjects, reported by some to be as common as 25% of those aged 40 years or over. Other research has concentrated on the apparently high prevalence of hyperactivity in boys with Down's syndrome, and the comparatively infrequent, albeit not negligible, occurrence of autism, given the level of learning disabilities that occurs in the syndrome.

Foetal alcohol syndrome

Foetal alcohol syndrome is caused by exposure to alcohol at critical periods of early gestation. The severity of the disorder varies according to the extent, timing and duration of alcohol exposure, as well as to other factors such as maternal diet, health and foetal circulation. Generally delayed development, short stature and midline facial anomalies are seen in the physical phenotype. Level of intellectual ability is variable, according to the severity of the condition: in most cases low/average intellect is more common than learning disabilities. A broad spectrum of psychopathology has been reported, most notably including general disinhibited behaviour with aggression, and many cases of attention-deficit hyperactivity disorder. Mood problems have also been reported, often in young children.

Fragile X syndrome

Fragile X syndrome affects between 1 in 1000 and 1 in 3000 children. The physical features are variable, with classically large, prominent or poorly folded ears, long face, and post-pubertal testicular enlargement in the majority of men. Intelligence is typically in the mild to moderate learning disabilities range. The behavioural phenotype is striking, with social anxiety and gaze avoidance, a characteristic language disorder, stereotypic movements and poor concentration. A considerable proportion of individuals in this diagnostic category additionally meet criteria for autism when young, and for ADHD in both childhood and adolescence. All of these features, including the degree of learning disabilities, are more pronounced in affected males than females.

Klinefelter syndrome

Klinefelter syndrome refers to all sex chromosome anomalies characterised by a surplus of X chromosomes in phenotypic males: 47,XXY; 48,XXYY; 48,XXXY; 46,XY/47,XXY are examples. The condition is not uncommon, estimated at around 1 in 500 to 1 in 1000 live male births. Of these, two-thirds are classical 47,XXY. Developmentally, from small size at birth, there is increased growth and attainment of puberty within normal limits. Intellectually, mean IQ is around 10 points below the general population average, with a range of between 60 and 130. Boys with the syndrome are introverted and quiet, and passive compared with their peers. By adolescence, a pattern of insecurity and apprehension predominates. However, there is much literature describing reports of psychopathic and aggressive traits in adulthood, while noting that these occur against a background of passivity. This may be explained by general difficulties in social adjustment and self-esteem.

Lesch-Nyhan syndrome

Lesch-Nyhan syndrome is an X-linked recessive disorder, involving a deficiency of an enzyme involved in purine metabolism (hypoxanthine phosphoribosyl transferase). Severe learning disabilities occur, with death in early adulthood being usual. Self-injurious behaviour is a prominent and severe feature. This has long been known to be uncontrollable, but non-volitional. The behaviour is unwelcome by affected individuals, who will cooperate with efforts made to prevent them injuring themselves, even including the controversial use of physical restraints that are employed in some cases where severe self-mutilation has occurred.

Noonan syndrome

Noonan syndrome is an autosomal dominant condition, variable in both its penetrance and expressivity. The variability of penetrance and expression is of such an extent that many cases are very mild, and probably go unrecognised. It is quite common, probably around 1 in 1000 live births. Physical features usually comprise short stature, a characteristic appearance (often likened to Turner Syndrome), and certain congenital heart defects, notably narrowing of the pulmonary valve. Studies of Noonan syndrome have reported stubborn, repetitive behaviour and poor socialisation, in the context of low normal intelligence or mild learning disabilities.

Phenylketonuria

Phenylketonuria (PKU) is an autosomal recessive disorder of metabolism with an incidence of around 1 in 10 000 live births. There are many versions of the genetic error that causes PKU, which therefore varies in occurence and severity in all respects, including intellegence and behaviour. Severity of the phenotype depends also on implementation of a special diet, low in phenylalanine. In untreated cases, almost all individuals fall into the moderate to severe learning disabilities range. Treated cases also commonly show low IQ, poor concentration, disinhibition, irritability, mannerisms, anxiety and socialisation problems.

Prader-Willi syndrome

About 70% of people with Prader-Willi syndrome have a deletion of paternal origin affecting the long arm of chromosome 15 at 15q11–q13. Most of the remaining people with the syndrome have maternal uniparental disomy for chromosome 15 (they inherit two chromosome 15s from their mother, instead of one from each parent). The fundamental genetic abnormality in Prader-Willi syndrome thus appears to be the absence of a paternal contribution to the relevant area of chromosome 15. A very small proportion of people have an abnormality in the imprinting centre on chromosome 15 (this 'marks' the chromosome as being of maternal or paternal origin, and alters the expression of genes) or a translocation (with an associated deletion).
As neonates, children with Prader-Willi syndrome are very hypotonic and feed poorly (most are tube fed). At around two years of age, there is a switch to over-eating (associated with delayed and incomplete satiation after eating), which may lead to morbid obesity. Affected adults are of short stature, with small hands and feet and characteristic dysmorphology. There is a failure of sexual development due to hypopituitary hypogonadism. A behaviour phenotype has been described: in addition to over-eating, adults may have a variety of sleep abnormalities, self-injury through skin-picking,

abnormally frequent and severe outbursts of temper, mood instability, repetitive speech and possibly a vulnerability to mood disorder and psychotic symptoms.

Rett syndrome

Rett syndrome occurs in around 1 in 10 000–15 000 female births. Recent reports suggest that the responsible gene has been identified, and the genetics are currently being delineated. The phenotype shows a four-stage progression, with:

1 early stagnation in development after initial progress;
2 a rapid deterioration with autistic-like picture generally by the age of three years;
3 a plateau stage; and
4 a late motor deterioration stage.

Motor disorder is prominent, with self-stimulation and self-hitting. By mid-childhood, some resumption in learning is possible, but most cases show a picture of mimicking cerebral palsy-type deformity by early adulthood.

Rubenstein-Taybi syndrome

Rubenstein-Taybi syndrome is a rare disorder of around 1 in 125 000 live births, with an equal gender ratio. The disorder is mostly sporadic. There have been some reports of identification of microdeletions, the significance of which is not yet established. Short stature, microcephaly, breathing difficulties and poor weight gain are prominent clinical problems. Poor concentration and distractibility is usual, as are moderate to severe learning disabilities, although some individuals have only mild learning disabilities. Self-stimulatory behaviours are common, as are other autistic-like behaviours, including hand-flapping, rocking and spinning. Resistance to environmental change is reported in over three-quarters, and intolerance to loud noises and self-injurious behaviours in about half. Mood disorders and temper tantrums appear to be more common than usual.

Smith-Magenis syndrome

Smith-Magenis syndrome is a rare condition, with an incidence of probably around 1 in 50 000 live births. There is a variable physical phenotype, most notably a 'cupid Bow' shape to the upper lip, broad face and nasal bridge, flat mid-face and a deep hoarse voice. Level of learning disabilities is also variable, from mild to severe, probably most often at moderate level. Behaviour, however, is dramatic, with a picture of self-injury that typically includes head-banging, self-hugging, wrist and hand-biting, and even pulling out finger and toe nails. Sensitivity to pain is thought to be impaired. Autism has been described in several people with the syndrome.

Sotos syndrome

Sotos syndrome is a sporadic, non-familial condition, sometimes called cerebral gigantism. Live birth frequency is unknown, largely because the features are so variable in expression. Sotos syndrome typically presents with a large head and body size, accelerated growth, advanced bone age, and a characteristic facial appearance with high forehead, prominent jaw, premature eruption of teeth and sparseness of hair, in addition to other eye and nasal findings. The main behavioural problems are in the area of aggression and emotional immaturity: given the large stature and appearance of the subjects, these problems assume greater importance than they might otherwise do.

Tuberous sclerosis

Tuberous sclerosis is an autosomal dominant disorder with variable expression; there is also a high incidence of new mutations (accounting for around 70% of cases). At least two variants exist, with aberrant genes on chromosomes 9 and 16 respectively. The condition is not uncommon, with a frequency of approximately 1 in 7000. The condition is sometimes characterised by the classic triad of epilepsy, learning disabilities and certain skin problems – notably the facial angiofibroma, but clinical features vary markedly. Other organ involvement is also common, notably kidney and cardiac abnormalities. The level of learning disabilities of affected individuals varies enormously, from severe learning disabilities through to average ability, according to brain involvement of blood vessel hamartomata and accompanying progressive changes. The most prominent psychological findings are of generally disturbed, distractible, explosive, aggressive and disinhibited behaviour, plus social and communication impairments, often amounting overall to a diagnosis of autism/ADHD. This may be closely related to brain pathology, and often proves difficult to treat: drug therapy is of limited success, although anti-epileptic drugs such as carbamazepine may be of some benefit.

Turner syndrome

Turner syndrome is a sporadic condition due to loss of all or part of one X chromosome. Half of women with the syndrome have classical 45X; others have mosaicism, isochrome Xq, ring forms, and other rarer forms. Physical features include short stature, usually obvious in the early school years (adult height is usually 120–150 cm) and premature ovarian failure *in utero*, giving rise to streak ovaries and hence lack of normal pubertal development. Other physical features include webbed neck, low posterior hairline, broad chest with wide-spaced nipples, increased carrying angle at the elbow, small nails and multiple pigmented naevi. The intelligence of affected women spans the normal range, but is more markedly reduced in those with ring chromosomes.
A cognitive profile including spacial deficit is recognised. Disorders of visuo-motor coordination, motor learning, visual memory, drawing, arithmetic and route-finding have been reported. The behavioural profile includes reports of difficulty in concentration, difficulty in peer relationships, eating difficulties, and depression in later life.

Velocardiofacial syndrome

The group of disorders subsumed under the category of velocardiofacial syndrome, which is probably underdiagnosed, has been shown to be due to defective gene material of chromosome 22q11, and has also been referred to by the term CATCH-22 syndrome (cardiac anomalies, abnormal face, thymus aplasia, cleft palate and hypocalcaemia). Individuals may have learning disabilities, although IQ is usually in the 90–100 range. Affected individuals may experience increased rates of psychiatric disorder, notably ADHD, autism and affective or psychotic disorders, in addition to learning disabilities.

Williams syndrome

Also often called idiopathic infantile hypercalcaemia, Williams syndrome is a fairly uncommon condition with an incidence of around 1 in 20 000 live births. Most cases are sporadic. The genetic basis of the disorder is a microdeletion on chromosome 7: 7q11.23, which disrupts the production of elastin, an important constituent of the body's connective tissue. Consequently, there are problems in the heart and arterial walls of affected people. More than 50% of affected individuals have moderate or severe learning disabilities, 40% have mild learning disabilities and 5% are of low average ability. Physical health screening is clearly a major issue for this multi-system disorder. The behavioural phenotype typically comprises: poor peer relations; outgoing, socially dis-inhibited reactions to others; excessively inappropriate affection towards adults (by affected children); and good expressive language with an odd character sometimes referred to as 'cocktail party' language. Hyperacusis, hypersensitivity to sound, is almost universal. It is also suggested that a capacity to over-empathise with the feelings of others is common, to an extent that can be quite emotionally disabling. In some, this seems to result in extreme emotional upsets: quite at odds with the 'easy-going' image people with Williams syndrome tend to give on first impressions. In addition, autism has been documented in subgroups of affected individuals.

APPENDIX 2: ICD–10 CHAPTERS OTHER THAN V – OTHER ASSOCIATED MEDICAL CONDITIONS

Chapter I: Certain infectious and parasitic diseases

- Congenital syphilis, unspecified [A50.9]
- Late syphilis, unspecified [A52.9]
- Slow virus infections of the central nervous system, unspecified [A81.9]
- Unspecified viral hepatitis [B19]
- Unspecified human immunodeficiency virus disease [B24]

Chapter II: Neoplasms

- Malignant neoplasm of brain, unspecified [C71.9]
- Lymphoid leukaemia, unspecified [C91.9]
- Myeloid leukaemia, unspecified [C92.9]
- Benign neoplasm of brain and other parts of the central nervous system [D33]

Chapter III: Diseases of the blood and blood-forming organs and certain diseases involving the immune mechanism

- Iron deficiency anaemia, unspecified [D50.9]
- Vitamin B12 deficiency anaemia, unspecified [D51.9]
- Folate deficiency anaemia, unspecified [D52.9]
- Thalassaemia, unspecified [D56.9]
- Sickle cell disease [D57]

Chapter IV: Endocrine, nutritional and metabolic diseases

- Iodine-deficiency-related thyroid disorders and allied conditions [E01]
- Hypothyroidism, unspecified [E03.9]
- Thyrotoxicosis, unspecified [E05.5]
- Insulin-dependent diabetes mellitus [E10]
- Non-insulin-dependent diabetes mellutis [E11]
- Hyperfunction of pituitary gland, unspecified [E22.9]

- Hypofunction and other disorders of pituitary gland [E23]
- Cushing's syndrome, unspecified [E24.9]
- Obesity, unspecified [E66.9]
- Disorders of porphyrin and bilirubin metabolism [E80]

Chapter VI: Diseases of the nervous system

- Intracranial abscess and granuloma [G06.0]
- Huntington's disease [G10]
- Hereditary ataxia, unspecified [G11.9]
- Parkinson's disease [G20]
- Secondary parkinsonism, unspecified [G21.9]
- Dystonia, unspecified [G24.9]
- Extrapyramidal and movement disorders, unspecified [G25.9]
- Multiple sclerosis [G35]
- Epilepsy
  - ➢ Partial idiopathic epilepsy and epileptic syndromes with seizures of localised onset [G40.0]
    Includes benign childhood epilepsy with centrotemporal EEG spikes, childhood epilepsy with occipital EEG paroxysms.
  - ➢ Partial symptomatic epilepsy and epileptic syndromes with simple partial seizures [G40.1]
    Includes episodes without alteration of consciousness, simple partial seizures developing into secondarily generalised seizures.
  - ➢ Partial symptomatic epilepsy and epileptic syndromes with complex partial epilepsy [G40.2]
    Includes episodes with alteration of consciousness often with automatism, complex partial epilepsy developing into secondarily generalised seizures.
  - ➢ Generalised idiopathic epilepsy and epileptic syndromes [G40.3]
    Includes benign myoclonic epilepsy in infancy, benign neonatal convulsions (familial), childhood absence epilepsy (pyknolepsy), epilepsy with tonic–clonic seizures on awakening, juvenile absence epilepsy, juvenile myoclonic epilepsy, non-specific epileptic seizures (atonic, clonic, myoclonic, tonic, tonic–clonic).
  - ➢ Other generalised epilepsy and epileptic syndromes [G40.4]
    Includes epilepsy with myoclonic absences, epilepsy with myoclonic–astatic seizures, infantile spasms, Lennox-Gastaut syndrome, Salaam attacks, West's

syndrome, symptomatic early myoclonic encephalopathy.
- ➢ Special epileptic syndromes [G40.5]
  Includes epilepsia partialis continua, epileptic seizures related to alcohol, drugs, hormonal changes, sleep deprivation, stress.
- ➢ Grand mal seizures, unspecified (with or without petit mal) [G40.6]
- ➢ Petit mal, unspecified, without grand mal seizures [G40.7]
- ➢ Other epilepsy [G40.8]
  Includes epilepsies and epileptic syndromes undetermined as to whether they are focal or generalised.
- ➢ Epilepsy, unspecified [G40.9]

> Note: An alternative classificatory system for epilepsy, produced by the International League Against Epilepsy, is outlined at the end of this Appendix.

- Status epilepticus, unspecified [G41.9]
- Migraine, unspecified [G43.9]
- Sleep disorders
  - ➢ Disorders of initiating and maintaining sleep (insomnias) [G47.0]; [equivalent to 780.52]
  - ➢ Disorders of excessive somnolence (hypersomnias) [G47.1]; [equivalent to 780.54]
  - ➢ Disorders of the sleep–wake schedule [G47.2]
  - ➢ Sleep apnoea [G47.3]; [equivalent to 780.59]
  - ➢ Narcolepsy and cataplexy [G47.4]; [equivalent to 347]
  - ➢ Other sleep disorders [G47.8]; [equivalent to 780.59]
    Includes Kleine-Levin syndrome.
- Cranial nerve disorder, unspecified [G52.9]
- Hereditary motor and sensory neuropathy [G60.0]
  Includes Charcot-Marie-Tooth disease.
- Myasthenia gravis [G70.0]
- Muscular dystrophy [G71.0]
- Cerebral palsy
  - ➢ Spastic cerebral palsy [G80.0]
  - ➢ Spastic diplegia [G80.1]
  - ➢ Infantile hemiplegia [G80.2]
  - ➢ Dyskinetic cerebral palsy [G80.3]
  - ➢ Ataxic cerebral palsy [G80.4]
  - ➢ Cerebral palsy, unspecified [G80.9]

- Hemiplegia, unspecified [G81.9]
- Paraplegia, unspecified [G82.2]
- Tetraplegia, unspecified [G82.5]
- Hydrocephalus, unspecified [G91.9]

Chapter VII: Diseases of the eye and adnexa

- Conjunctivitis, unspecified [H10.9]
- Corneal scar and opacity, unspecified [H17.9]
- Keratoconus [H18.6]
- Senile cataract, unspecified [H25.9]
- Infantile, juvenile and presenile cataract [H26.0]
- Cataract, unspecified [H26.9]
- Congenital cataract [Q12]
- Hereditary retinal dystrophy [H35.5]
  Includes retinitis pigmentosis.
- Glaucoma, unspecified [H40.9]
- Paralytic strabismus, unspecified [H49.9]
- Hypermetropia [H52.0]
- Myopia [H52.1]
- Astigmatism [H52.2]
- Blindness, both eyes [H54.0]
- Blindness, one eye, low vision other eye [H54.1]
- Low vision, both eyes [H54.2]
- Unqualified visual loss, both eyes [H54.3]
- Blindness, one eye [H54.4]
- Low vision, one eye [H54.5]
- Unqualified visual loss, one eye [H54.6]
- Unspecified visual loss [H54.7]
- Nystagmus and other irregular eye movements [H55]

Chapter VIII: Diseases of the ear and mastoid process

- Otitis externa, unspecified [H60.9]
- Impacted cerumen [H61.2]
- Otitis media, unspecified [H66.9]
- Conductive hearing loss, unspecified [H90.2]
- Sensorineural hearing loss, unspecified [H90.5]
- Mixed conductive and sensorineural loss, unspecified [H90.8]

Chapter IX: Diseases of the circulatory system

- Multiple valve disease, unspecified [I08.9]
- Essential hypertension [I10]

- Secondary hypertension, unspecified [I15.9]
- Angina pectoris, unspecified [I20.9]
- Acute myocardial infarction, unspecified [I21.9]
- Old myocardial infarction [I25.2]
- Left ventricular failure [I50.1]
- Subarachnoid haemorrhage, unspecified [I60.9]
- Intracerebral haemorrhage, unspecified [I61.9]
- Cerebral infarction, unspecified [I63.9]
- Stroke, not specified as haemorrhage or infarction [I64]
- Raynaud's syndrome [I73.0]
- Peripheral vascular disease, unspecified [I73.9]
- Haemorrhoids [I84]

Chapter X: Diseases of the respiratory system

- Influenza, virus not identified [J11]
- Viral pneumonia, unspecified [J12.9]
- Pneumonia, due to *Streptococcus pneumoniae* [J13]
- Pneumonia, due to *Haemophilus influenzae* [J14]
- Bacterial pneumonia, unspecified [J15.9]
- Pneumonia, unspecified [J18.9]
- Acute bronchitis, unspecified [J20.9]
- Allergic rhinitis, due to pollen [J30.0]
- Allergic rhinitis, unspecified [J30.4]
- Unspecified chronic bronchitis [J42]
- Emphysema [J43]
- Asthma, unspecified [J45.9]

Chapter XI: Diseases of the digestive system

- Gastric ulcer [K25]
- Duodenal ulcer [K26]
- Peptic ulcer, site unspecified [K27]
- Gastritis, unspecified [K29.7]
- Dyspepsia [K30]

Chapter XII: Diseases of the skin and subcutaneous tissue

- Impetigo (any organism) (any site) [L01.0]
- Cellulitis, unspecified [L03.9]
- Other atopic dermatitis [L20.8]
  Includes eczema.
- Unspecified contact dermatitis, unspecified cause [L25.9]
- Psoriasis, unspecified [L40.9]

Chapter XIII: Diseases of the musculoskeletal system and connective tissue

- Arthritis, unspecified [M13.9]
- Primary generalised osteoarthritis [M15.0]
- Acquired deformity of limb, unspecified [M21.9]
- Systemic lupus erythematosus, unspecified [M32]
- Systemic involvement of connective tissue, unspecified [M35.9]
- Unspecified kyphosis [M40.2]
- Lordosis, unspecified [M40.5]
- Scoliosis, unspecified [M41.9]
  Includes kyphoscoliosis.
- Torticollis [M43.6]
- Low back pain [M54.5]
- Unspecified osteoporosis with pathological fracture [M80.9]
- Osteoporosis without pathological fracture, unspecified [M81.9]

Chapter XIV: Diseases of the genitourinary system

- Cystitis, unspecified [N30.9]
- Urinary tract infection, site not specified [N39.0]
- Primary amenorrhoea [N91.0]
- Secondary amenorrhoea [N91.1]
- Oligomenorrhoea, unspecified [N91.5]
- Excessive and frequent menstruation with regular cycle [N92.0]
- Excessive and frequent menstruation with irregular cycle [N92.1]
- Premenstrual tension syndrome [N94.3]; [equivalent to premenstrual dysphoric disorder]
- Dysmenorrhoea, unspecified [N94.6]

Chapter XVII: Congenital malformations, deformities, and chromosomal abnormalities

- Spina bifida, unspecified [Q05.9]
- Congenital ectropion [Q10.1]
- Congenital entropion [Q10.2]
- Other anophthalmos [Q11.1]
- Microphthalmos [Q11.2]
- Congenital cataract [Q12.0]
- Congenital corneal opacity [Q13.3]
- Congenital malformation of eye, unspecified [Q15.9]

- Congenital malformation of ear causing impairment of hearing, unspecified [Q16.9]
- Congenital malformation of ear, unspecified [Q17.9]
- Congenital malformation of cardiac chambers and connections, unspecified [Q20.9]
- Ventricular septal defect [Q21.0]
- Atrial septal defect [Q21.1]
- Atrio-ventricular septal defect [Q22.2]
- Tetralogy of Fallot [Q21.3]
- Other congenital malformations of cardiac septa [Q21.9] Includes Eisenmenger's syndrome.
- Congenital malformation of cardiac septum, unspecified [Q21.9]
- Pulmonary valve atresia [Q22.0]
- Congenital pulmonary valve stenosis [Q22.1]
- Congenital pulmonary valve insufficiency [Q22.2]
- Ebstein's anomaly [Q22.5]
- Congenital malformation of tricuspid valve, unspecified [Q22.9]
- Congenital malformation of aortic and mitral valves, unspecified [Q23.9]
- Congenital malformation of heart, unspecified [Q24.9]
- Congenital malformation of great arteries, unspecified [Q25.9]
- Cleft palate, unspecified, bilateral [Q35.8]
- Cleft palate, unspecified, unilateral [Q35.9]
- Cleft lip, bilateral [Q36.0]
- Cleft lip, unilateral [Q36.1]
- Unspecified cleft palate with cleft lip, bilateral [Q37.8]
- Unspecified cleft palate with cleft lip, unilateral [Q37.9]
- Hypospadias, unspecified [Q54.9]
- Undescended testicle, unspecified [Q53.9]
- Cystic kidney disease, unspecified [Q61.9]
- Talipes equino-varus [Q66.0]
- Congenital deformity of feet, unspecified [Q66.9]
- Congenital pes planus (flat foot) [Q66.5]
- Congenital pes cavus [Q66.7]
- Pectus excavatum (congenital funnel chest) [Q67.5]
- Pectus carinatum (congenital pigeon chest) [Q67.7]
- Congenital deformity of spine [Q67.5] Includes congenital scoliosis.
- Congenital deformity of sternocleidomastoid muscle [Q75.9] Includes congenital torticollis.

- Polydactyly, unspecified [Q69.9]
- Syndactyly, unspecified [Q70.9]
- Congenital malformations of skull and face bones, unspecified [Q75.9]
- Situs inversus [Q89.3]

Chapter XVIII: Symptoms, signs and abnormal clinical and laboratory findings, not elsewhere classified

- Nausea and vomiting [R11]
- Faecal incontinence [R15]
- Other and unspecified abnormalities of gait and mobility [R26.8]
- Unspecified urinary incontinence [R32]
- Dysphasia and aphasia [R47.0]
- Dysarthria [R47.1]
- Cachexia [R64]

Chapter XIX: Injury, poisoning and certain other consequences of external cause

- Concussion [S06.0]
- Diffuse brain injury [S06.2]
- Focal brain injury [S06.3]
- Traumatic subdural haemorrhage [S06.5]
- Traumatic subarachnoid haemorrhage [S06.6]
- Intracranial injury with prolonged coma [S06.7]
- Neglect or abandonment [T74.0]
- Physical abuse [T74.1]; [equivalent to V61.21, V61.1]
  Includes battered baby syndrome.
- Sexual abuse [T74.2]; [equivalent to V61.21, V61.1]
- Psychological abuse [T74.3]
- Other maltreatment syndromes (mixed form) [T74.8]
- Maltreatment syndrome, unspecified [T74.9]
  Includes effects of abuse of adult not otherwise specified or effects of child abuse not otherwise specified.
- Motion sickness [T75.3]

Chapter XX: External causes of morbidity and mortality

This chapter permits the classification of environmental events and circumstances as the cause of injury, poisoning and other adverse effects. Where a code from this section is applicable, it should be used in addition to a code from another chapter of ICD–10, indicating the nature of the condition.

- Pedestrian injured in unspecified transport accident [V09.9]
- Car occupant (any) injured in unspecified traffic accident [V49.9]
- Person injured in unspecified vehicle accident [V89.9]
- Unspecified transport accident [V99]
- Accidental poisoning by and exposure to other and unspecified drugs, medicaments and biological substances [X44]
- Accidental poisoning by and exposure to other and unspecified chemicals and noxious substances [X49]
- Sexual assault by bodily force [Y05]
- Neglect and abandonment [Y06]
- Other maltreatment syndromes [Y07]
  Includes mental cruelty, physical abuse, sexual abuse, torture.
- Drugs, medications and biological substances causing adverse effects in therapeutic use
  - Anti-epileptics and anti-parkinsonism drugs [Y46]
  - Sedatives, hypnotics and anxiolytic drugs [Y47]
  - Tricyclic and tetracyclic antidepressants [Y49.0]
  - Monoamine oxidase inhibitor antidepressants [Y49.1]
  - Other and unspecified antidepressants [Y49.2]
  - Phenothiazine antipsychotics and neuroleptics [Y49.3]
  - Butyrophenones and thioxanthene neuroleptics [Y49.5]
  - Other antipsychotics and neuroleptics [Y49.5]
  - Other psychotropics drugs, not elsewhere specified [Y49.8]
  - Psychotropic drugs, unspecified [Y49.9]

The International League Against Epilepsy classification of epilepsy and syndromes

- Localisation-related (focal, partial) epilepsies and epileptic syndromes
  - *Idiopathic* (with age-related onset)
    Includes benign Rolandic epilepsy, benign childhood epilepsy with centrotemporal spikes, childhood epilepsy with occipital paroxysms, primary reading epilepsy.
  - *Symptomatic*
    Includes chronic progressive epilepsia partialis continus of childhood (Kojewnikow syndrome), syndromes characterised by seizures with specific

modes of precipitation (e.g. partial seizures following acquired lesions, usually involving tactile or proprioceptive stimuli; partial seizures precipitated by sudden arousal or startle epilepsy), syndromes that result from seizures arising from a specific part of the brain, but which may have diverse but defined aetiologies (e.g. temporal lobe epilepsies; frontal lobe epilepsies; parietal lobe epilepsies; occipital lobe epilepsies).

> *Cryptogenic*

- Generalised epilepsies and syndromes
  > *Idiopathic* (with age-related onset)
  Includes benign neonatal familial convulsions, benign neonatal convulsions, benign myoclonic epilepsy in infancy, childhood absence epilepsy (pyknolepsy), juvenile absence epilepsy, juvenile myoclonic epilepsy (impulsive petit mal), epilepsy with grand mal seizures on awakening, other generalized epilepsies (not defined above), epilepsies with seizures precipitated by specific modes of activation.

  > *Cryptogenic*
  Includes West syndrome (infantile spasms, Blitz-Nick-Salaam Krampfe), Lennox-Gastaut syndrome, epilepsy with myoclonic–astatic seizures, epilepsy with myoclonic absences.

  > *Symptomatic*
  Includes non-specific aetiology (e.g. early myoclonic encephalopathy; early infantile epileptic encephalopathy with suppression-burst electroencephalogram; other symptomatic generalised epilepsies not defined above), specific syndromes (e.g. diseases in which seizures are a presenting or predominant feature, such as Lafora body disease).

- Epilepsies and epileptic syndromes undetermined whether focal or generalised
  Includes neonatal seizures, severe myoclonic epilepsy in infancy, epilepsy with continuous spike-waves during slow-wave sleep, acquired epileptic aphasia (Landau-Kleffner syndrome), other undetermined epilepsies not defined above.

- Special syndromes
  Includes situation-related seizures (e.g. febrile convulsions, isolated seizures or isolated status epilepticus, seizures occurring only when there is an acute metabolic or toxic event).

APPENDIX 3: ICD–10 CHAPTER XXI – FACTORS INFLUENCING HEALTH STATUS AND CONTACT WITH HEALTH SERVICES

The ICD–10 manuals advise that this chapter should not be used for international comparison. These codes are for occasions when circumstances other than a disease, injury or external cause classifiable to A00–Y89 are recorded as 'diagnoses' or 'problems', for example when some circumstance or problem is present that influences the person's health status, but is not in itself a current illness or injury. As such, this explains the reason for contact with the health services of a person not currently sick, or the circumstances in which the person is receiving care at that particular time, or classifies factors otherwise having some bearing on that person's care.

- Problems related to education and literacy
  - Schooling unavailable and unattainable [Z55.1]
  - Under-achievement in school [Z55.3]
  - Educational maladjustment and discord with teachers and classmates [Z55.4]
  - Problems related to education and literacy, unspecified [Z55.9]

- Problems related to employment and unemployment
  - Unemployment, unspecified [Z56.0]
  - Change of job [Z56.1]
  - Stressful work schedule [Z56.3]
  - Discord with boss and workmates [Z56.4]
  - Other and unspecified problems related to employment [Z56.7]; [equivalent to V62.3]

- Problems related to housing and economic circumstances
  - Homelessness [Z59.0]
  - Inadequate housing [Z59.1]
  - Discord with neighbours, lodgers and landlord [Z59.2]

- ➢ Problems related to living in residential institutions [Z59.3]
- ➢ Extreme poverty [Z59.5]
- ➢ Low income [Z59.6]
- ➢ Problem related to housing and economic circumstances, unspecified [Z59.9]

- Problems related to social environment
  - ➢ Problems of adjustment to life-cycle transitions [Z60.0]; [equivalent to V62.89]
  - ➢ Atypical parenting situation [Z60.1]
  - ➢ Living alone [Z60.2]
  - ➢ Acculturation difficulty [Z60.3]; [equivalent to V62.4]
  - ➢ Social exclusion and rejection [Z60.4]
  - ➢ Target of perceived adverse discrimination and persecution [Z60.5]
  - ➢ Problems related to social environment, unspecified [Z60.9]

- Problems related to negative life events in childhood
  - ➢ Loss of love relationship in childhood [Z61.0]
  - ➢ Removal from home in childhood [Z61.1]
  - ➢ Altered pattern of family relationships in childhood [Z61.2]
  - ➢ Events resulting in loss of self-esteem in childhood [Z61.3]
  - ➢ Problems related to alleged sexual abuse of child by person within primary support group [Z61.4]
  - ➢ Problems related to alleged sexual abuse of child by person outside primary support group [Z61.5]
  - ➢ Problems related to alleged physical abuse of child [Z61.6]
  - ➢ Personal frightening experience in childhood [Z61.7]
  - ➢ Other negative life events in childhood [Z61.8]
  - ➢ Negative life events in childhood, unspecified [Z61.9]

- Other problems related to upbringing
  - ➢ Inadequate parental supervision and control [Z62.0]
  - ➢ Parental overprotection [Z62.1]
  - ➢ Institutional upbringing [Z62.2]
  - ➢ Hostility towards and scapegoating of child [Z62.3]
  - ➢ Emotional neglect of child [Z62.4]
  - ➢ Other problems related to neglect in upbringing [Z62.5]
  - ➢ Inappropriate parental pressure and other abnormal qualities of upbringing [Z62.6]

- ➤ Other specified problems related to upbringing [Z62.8]
- ➤ Problems related to upbringing, unspecified [Z62.9]

- Other problems related to primary support group, including family circumstances
  - ➤ Problems in relationship with spouse or partner [Z63.0]
  - ➤ Problems in relationship with parents and in-laws [Z63.1]
  - ➤ Inadequate family support [Z63.2]
  - ➤ Absence of family member [Z63.3]
  - ➤ Disappearance and death of family member [Z63.4]; [equivalent to V62.82]
  - ➤ Disruption of family by separation and divorce [Z63.5]
  - ➤ Dependent relative needing care at home [Z63.6]
  - ➤ Other stressful life events affecting family and household [Z63.7]
  - ➤ Other specified problems related to primary support group [Z63.8]
  - ➤ Problems related to primary support group, unspecified [Z63.9]

- Problems related to certain psychosocial circumstances [Z64]
  - ➤ Problems related to unwanted pregnancy [Z64.0]
  - ➤ Seeking and accepting physical, nutritional and chemical interventions known to be hazardous and harmful [Z64.2]
  - ➤ Seeking and accepting behavioural and psychological interventions known to be hazardous and harmful [Z64.3]
  - ➤ Discord with counsellors [Z64.4]

- Problems related to other psychosocial circumstances
  - ➤ Conviction in civil and criminal proceedings without imprisonment [Z65.0]
  - ➤ Imprisonment and other incarceration [Z65.1]
  - ➤ Problems related to release from prison [Z65.2]
  - ➤ Problems related to other legal circumstances [Z65.3]
  - ➤ Victim of crime and terrorism (including torture) [Z65.4]
  - ➤ Exposure to disaster, war and other hostilities [Z65.5]
  - ➤ Other specified problem related to psychosocial circumstances [Z65.8]
  - ➤ Problem related to unspecified psychosocial circumstances [Z65.9]

- Problems relating to lifestyle
  - Tobacco use [Z72.0]
  - Alcohol use [Z72.1]
  - Drug use [Z72.2]
  - Lack of physical exercise [Z72.3]
  - Inappropriate diet and eating habits [Z72.4]
  - High-risk sexual behaviour [Z72.5]
  - Gambling and betting [Z72.6]
  - Other problems related to lifestyle [Z72.8]; [equivalent to V71.0, V71.02]
  - Problems related to lifestyle, unspecified [Z72.9]

- Problems related to life-management difficulty
  - Burn-out [Z73.0]
  - Accentuation of personality traits [Z73.1]
  - Lack of relaxation or leisure [Z73.2]
  - Stress, not elsewhere classified [Z73.3]
  - Inadequate social skills, not elsewhere classified [Z73.4]
  - Social role conflict, not elsewhere classified [Z73.5]
  - Limitation of activities due to disability [Z73.6]
  - Other problems related to life-management difficulty [Z73.8]
  - Problems related to life-management difficulty, unspecified [Z73.9]

- Problems related to medical facilities and other health care
  - Person awaiting admission to adequate facility elsewhere [Z75.1]
  - Other waiting period for an investigation and treatment [Z75.2]
  - Holiday relief care [Z75.5]
  - Unspecified problem related to medical facilities and other health care [Z75.9]

- Family history of mental and behavioural disorders
  - Family history of learning disabilities [Z81.0]
  - Family history of alcohol abuse [Z81.1]
  - Family history of other psychoactive substance abuse [Z81.3]
  - Family history of other mental and behavioural disorders [Z81.8]

- Family history of certain disabilities and chronic diseases leading to disablement [Z82]
  - ➢ Family history of epilepsy and other diseases of the nervous system [Z82.0]
  - ➢ Family history of congenital malformations, deformities and chromosomal abnormalities [Z82.7]

- Personal history of risk-factors, not elsewhere classified
  - ➢ Personal history of non-compliance with medical treatment and regimen [Z91.1]; [equivalent to V15.81]
  - ➢ Personal history of psychological trauma, not elsewhere classified [Z91.4]
  - ➢ Personal history of other specified risk factors, not elsewhere classified [Z91.8]

INDEX